CARRIERS
OF THE GLORY

REACHING FOR THE
GREATER IN YOU

DR. JERONN C. WILLAMS, I

CARRIERS
OF THE GLORY

REACHING FOR THE
GREATER IN YOU

DR. JERONN C. WILLAMS, I

MEWE
Lithonia, GA

Scripture references are taken from various versions and
translations of the Holy Bible. Pronouns for referring to the Father,
Son and Holy Spirit are capitalized intentionally and the words
satan and devil are never capitalized.

Publisher:
MEWE, LLC
www.mewellc.com

First Edition
ISBN: 9781732432710

Printed in the United States of America.

Thank you to the following individuals who without their support and contributions this book would not have been written:

First and foremost, to my Lord and Savior Jesus the Christ for choosing me.

To my darling wife, Dr. LaToya K. Williams, thank you for your enduring patience.

To my son, Jeronn C. Williams II, thank you for letting dad do all that dad does.

To my dad, the late Elder James H. Williams, I miss you!

To my mom and sisters, Elder Donna J. Williams, Sheronn Williams and LeShonn Miller (Robert), for always caring and standing with me.

To my church, New Life International Family Church, for embracing me.

To my reformation, Breath of Life Fellowship, for believing in me.

To my J.C. Williams Ministries staff for pushing me to the world.

To all of my comrades and co-laborers in the Gospel of Jesus Christ, may you be strengthened and encouraged in your assignment.

TABLE OF CONTENTS

ACKNOWLEDGEMENTS

I have had the privilege of being impacted, shaped, and molded by some phenomenal men and women. In August of 1972, the late Apostle Arturo Skinner stopped my mom in a live service during his Annual Deliverance Convention and said "Daughter, are you ready for that baby boy" and she said, "no sir, I'm not expecting". He continued, "By this time next year you will have a baby boy" and continued prophesying over my life. I had the privilege of being pastored for 21 years of my life by the late Apostle Charles O. Miles of Ecorse, Michigan, who served not only as my pastor, but also as my Elijah.

The late Apostle Richard D. Henton of Chicago, Illinois, who unknowingly inspired me in the preaching of God's Word and in the demonstration of the Gifts of the Spirit. The late Apostle Lobias Murray of Dallas, Texas took me in as a Godson after the passing of my pastor and gave me the privilege of laying his hands on me in ordination.

Archbishop Lawrence Langston of Tampa, Florida saw enough in me to consecrate me Bishop in 2007 and continues to play an integral role in my life and ministry. Bishop Quincy Lavelle Carswell embraced me and continues to encourage, strengthen, and stand by me in life as well as ministry.

Bishop Liza Hickman who is a phenomenal woman of God and a safe place at all times! Dr. Vivian Chillis Bryant who took me in high school and walked me into Morehouse College. The most valuable man in my life, the late Elder James H. Williams, my father, who taught me how to love, established in me a work ethic, showed me how to live life fully and with fulfillment, and remains my hero!

And finally, to my son, Jeronn C. Williams, II, who

inspires me every day to be better in every area of my life; my man, like 150 grand!

I dedicate this book to these men and women who taught me each in their own way how to "Carry the Glory."

FOREWORD

Bishop Dr. Jerron Williams is one of God's cutting-edge generals. His incredible understanding, revelation and delivery of the Word as well as his diverse music talents makes him more than accepted in most circles and extremely dangerous to the kingdom of darkness.

In today's fast-moving world, it's sometimes difficult to stay focused on one's destiny. Great athletes must be focused to win. NASCAR drivers must stay focused to drive at over 200 m.p.h. God has given Bishop the insight to operate in a higher dimension. The world around him moves at blinding speed, but he remains focused on the mandate given to him. His destiny is sure. His commitment is strong. His character is branded with integrity.

He is not only a minister for and in the Kingdom of God, he is a mentor, business and wealth building instructor, and motivational coach. His history of faith has given him credentials that surpass many that he is connected with. He is respected and revered by his peers who acknowledge that he has wisdom beyond his years which has been proven time and again. I am honored to call him "Son." He has walked in my shadow, now I find myself walking in his. To God Be the Glory!

Archbishop General, Dr. Lawrence Langston
Tabernacle Bible College Christian University
Coalition of Transitional Leaders
Tampa, Florida U.S.A.

PREFACE

We are living in the greatest generation that has ever graced the face of the earth. This generation is postured in time to produce the most powerful shift towards God that has ever occurred. As we explore scripture, we see that Noah was unable to get the people on the ark; Moses led millions out of Egypt, but only one of them journeyed into Canaan; Nehemiah could only get a remnant of the people to rebuild the wall; the prophets could only bring parts of nations to repentance. But the hour that this generation is currently occupying is potent with possibilities.

We must therefore, embrace the concept that we are not to reinvent the wheel, but to update it for maximum efficiency. The glory of God, embodied in the Ark of the Covenant, was entrusted to Priests to be transported. It was the representation of the presence, protection, and power of God amongst His people. The Bible teaches that we all in Christ are a royal priesthood. Therefore, the glory of God is now entrusted to every believer to carry. Just as it did then, it will yet demonstrate the presence, protection, and power of God in this current time. History is not just to be remembered and understood, but also to be built upon to produce strength, understanding, and clarity in the present to build a greater future.

We must understand that we are called in this hour to be *Carriers of the Glory*!

Jeronn C. Williams, I

1 The Riches of His Glory

Whereof I am made a minister, according to the dispensation of God which is given to me for you, to fulfill the word of God; Even the mystery which hath been hid from ages and from generations, but now is made manifest to His saints: To whom God would make known what is the riches of the glory of this mystery among the Gentiles; which is Christ in you, the hope of glory (Colossians 1:25–27).

From the beginning of the promises of God until the revelation of Christ, the great mystery of the Jewish faith was that God would alter His modus operandi toward His children: how God operated with those who believed in Him would change so that His Spirit would no longer simply come *upon* them, but rather He would make His abode *in* them.

This phenomenal mystery was foreshadowed in His Word, promised long before Christ came and the Holy Spirit descended. The old prophets proclaimed it would happen, even when they did not fully understand what they prophesied. Isaiah, one of the main prophets who foretold the Savior's arrival, revealed vital components of the Messiah's characteristics: *"and His name shall be called Wonderful, Counsellor, the mighty God, the everlasting Father, the Prince of Peace"* (Isaiah 9:6b).

Because the prophets told us much regarding the coming Messiah, that was not the truly hidden aspect of the mystery yet to unfold. Instead, the striking revelation to come was how He would live inside those whom He did not initially choose as His people.

The incredible truth behind the mystery is that God always planned to extend Himself beyond His immediate family, Israel. He would not limit His goodness to a few; He would not limit His glory to only those who were descendants of Abraham in the flesh. God would instead allow non-Jews all over the world to experience adoption into the spiritual family of Abraham. He waited for the time when the Messiah, Emmanuel—God with us, God in the flesh—would say to all peoples, *"Whosoever will, let him come."*

The invitation extended far beyond the Israelites: God offered it to anyone at all who desired to find Him. *"Come unto Me, all ye that labor and are heavy laden, and I will give you rest"* (Matthew 11:28). The phenomenal truth behind the mystery of Christ was that God would throw open the doors of salvation to admit the whole world, to allow those beyond His special people to be carriers of His glory.

What a privilege it is to be an adopted child and a carrier of the glory of God! Sometimes, we fail to recognize that we are God-carriers. Because we do not focus on what has entered into us, but rather on what is external, we don't act in a way respectful of what we carry inside us. The mystery revealed is not found in the office of apostle, prophet, evangelist, pastor, or teacher. It is not found in the gift of miracles or the gift of tongues and interpretations, or any of the other ministries or gifts of the Spirit. The real revelation is of Who is in us—Christ (the Christos).

The anointing of God lives within us; we are carriers of the Glory of God.

What Is the Glory?

Often, we tend to think that only bishops, apostles, and the great people of God who work miracles are the carriers of the glory. Yet, the mystery teaches us that whoever Christ has saved is a carrier of that glory.

What then is the glory? The glory is the honor, the abundance, the riches, the splendor, the dignity, the reputation, and the reverence of God. Glory is not a mere feeling, like a desire that makes you shout and dance. It is not just Shekinah. It is not limited to what makes you fall prostrate. There is a glory that will knock you off your feet, that will make you run the race when you do not feel like it, and that will make you shout, "Hallelujah!" There is a glory that stirs something within you and compels you to respond to it, but it is not limited to a feeling.

The glory of God is not restricted to the atmosphere that circumstances create, because the glory living in you creates an atmosphere wherever you go. If you are a carrier of the glory, no oppressive or weary atmosphere can defeat your spirit. What the Old Testament priests carried on their shoulders in the Ark of the Covenant, you carry within yourself—in your inner man. What David tried to transport into Zion was only foreshadowing the glory of God that would inhabit each of His children.

We often want the wrong things from this glory. In our present generation, we want to look appealing and empowered. We want to look distinguished and distinct for our own sakes. The truth of the matter is this: when the real glory comes into your life, it will disrupt your outward presentation and the esteem you receive from others.

When the real glory enters your life, you will surrender many comforts you clung to before you had something more fulfilling. God's glory is not exhibited in external factors. Attaining glory may make your hair a mess, your shoes worn out, your best outfits a wreck, and your appearance sweaty and lowly. His glory is not concerned with the outward man; it concerns itself with the internal, and it adjusts the inward individual to reflect its characteristics.

Glory, in its full translation, means honor, abundance, riches, splendor, dignity, reputation, and reverence. When you are a glory carrier, you bear all those things for the sake of Christ. To carry the glory of God means you carry the wealth of God. This wealth is not reduced to financial standing—rather, it is the resources and abundance of God that rests with you. His dignity and honor, the weightiness and richness of His Spirit, are to be

4

upheld by us, since He has filled us with His glory. Your role is to reflect the wealth and honor of Christ as you carry His glory within the temple of your body.

The Truth of the God-Man

God! The cattle on a thousand hills belong to Him, who, if He ever hungered, would never need to look beyond the feasts available to Him. God! The Creator and Sustainer of the universe, who set the night and day. The sun obeys His word, to rise every morning in the east and set every evening in the west. God!

The Master of the earth, who compels the seed to sprout and produce its harvest. God! When there was no light, He gave light to the universe and the very face of our world. In His splendor and excellence,

He poured Himself into Christ until the fullness of God existed within the physical body of the Christos. This is the truth that absolutely had to come to pass, so that the Anointed One could save His people from their sins.

Jesus Christ modeled the fullness of God and the fullness of humanity: He was fully God and fully Man at once. *"And the Word was made flesh, and dwelt among us (and we beheld His glory, the glory as of the only begotten of the Father), full of grace and truth"* (John 1:14). He was not so much man that He could not be God, and yet not so much God that He could not be man.

Jesus never gave up His divinity when He came, but He still became wholly Man. Philippians 2:6–8 described Jesus' ministry as thus:

> *"Who, being in the form of God, thought it not robbery to be equal with God: but made Himself of no reputation, and took upon Him the form of a servant, and was made in the likeness of men: and*

being found in fashion as a man, He humbled Himself, and became obedient unto death, even the death of the cross."

If He had not become man, He would not have been able to save mankind—but without maintaining His place in the Godhead, He could not have brought us salvation.

Abraham sought salvation, Isaac and Jacob sought it, Moses and Joshua tried to lay hold of it, and Isaiah and Jeremiah longed for it, but not one of them could save man as he needed to be saved.

For salvation, God knew He could not simply give mankind His Law and expect them to adjust their sinful natures by it and save themselves. He had to give mankind a Savior who experienced the same trials and limitations that they did. The Book of Romans explains the need of the God-Man to undo the harm of Adam's transgression: *"For as by one man's disobedience many were made sinners, so by the obedience of one shall many be made righteous"* (Romans 5:19). He could not be only a man, because then, He would have been subjected to Adam's curse—but mankind needed a Savior made especially for them.

The God-Man represents more than salvation: He is also the model of our living. His actions are not just for us to admire, but for us to emulate. He taught us through example to live as a reflection of the glory of God, to learn how to live the way God desires of us. *"As the Father hath loved Me, so have I loved you: continue ye in My love. If ye keep My commandments, ye shall abide in My love; even as I have kept My Father's commandments, and abide in His love"* (John 15:9–10).

Jesus was the initial carrier of glory, the first person indwelled of God. As recorded in John 10:30, He told the Jews, *"I and My Father are one."* Many theologians and scholars want to insist on a doctrine that says Jesus and the Father are not the same individual, filled with the same purpose, but they are twisting the Scripture and denying the very root of salvation. It was God in Christ who worked our salvation. Jesus further expounded this point: *"he that hath seen Me hath seen the Father; and how sayest thou then, 'Show us the Father'"* (John 14:9b).

He acknowledged again and again that He bore the glory of God within Him, but His actions showed more than a simple inward dwelling of God: He showed His oneness with God the Father by His submission to the Father's will. He had no agenda separate from the Father's; He had no lifestyle that contradicted the will of the Father. He lived to do His Father's will, and through that He remained one with Him. The same is applicable to us: whatever we submit ourselves to, we become one with that thing.

How many of us can honestly say that our lives are modelled after His so well that those who see us have seen a glimpse of the Father? We struggle because we have not fully submitted ourselves to the Spirit that indwells us, that we carry inside ourselves.

The only reason we have lost sight of the true value of what's in us is because we focus too much on what is around us. We want to achieve what the people around us achieved and to indulge in the entertainment and pleasures of this world, instead of consulting the glory we carry. Succumbing to ambition means you sacrifice fulfillment for temporal attainment. Even if you have sixteen doctoral degrees, own twenty-five companies, and make five hundred million a year, those exterior accomplishments mean nothing in the end. You won't be fulfilled. You can have a jet at the airport, you can have a helicopter in your backyard, and you can have a train to take you from your mansion to the helicopter that will take you to your private strip at the airport, but even though the plane can take you anywhere you want to go in the world, for however long you want to go, it will not bring you fulfillment. The more you get, the more you want; the more you want, the less you pursue what you need.

Truth be told, some of us cannot be rich in this life. Some of us won't make money because we focus on stupid things and remain broke. Some of us won't make money because nothing seems to work out right. However, when you are bored and broke, you have limitations, boundaries set by what you cannot afford to do. When you are bored and rich, everything the world has to offer is at your disposal. This is why the rich and famous engage in so much scandalous behavior, and why Jesus told His disciples, *"It is easier for a camel to go through the eye of a needle, than for a rich man to enter into the kingdom of God"* (Matthew 19:24b).

Many times, it is not that God does not want you to be rich, but that He does not want you to succumb to the world and go to hell. He does not want earthly riches to take you out of the Kingdom. You should not concern yourself with financial status, but rather your richness in Him. Pray for maturity in the spirit rather than for money. The prayer most beneficial to you is that you would grow in Him, from a babe in need of milk to a mature, submissive adult.

E.M. Bounds put it this way: "Men who belong to God are obliged to pray. They are not obliged to grow rich, nor make money. They are not obliged to have large success in business. These are incidental, occasional, merely nominal, as far as integrity to heaven and loyalty to God are concerned. Material successes are immaterial to God." He well understood the purpose of earthly riches and how little God thinks of them. Bounds insisted on forgetting the greed and desire for earthly riches, and instead pursuing on earth the riches of heaven. "[Riches] are not sources of reputation nor elements of character in the heavenly estimates. But to pray, to really pray, is the source of revenue, the basis of reputation, and the element of character in the estimation of God."

When you have proven yourself in the little things, then God can entrust you with the great things of His Kingdom. If He can discipline you and grow you so that you carry His glory honorably, then more will be added unto you. Prove yourself in your current state, and God will give you the true riches of the Kingdom. This mindset is the first part in unveiling the glory within you: the glory expressed in stewardship.

The Stewardship of Glory

Stewardship is a privilege we are honored with when we receive God's glory in us. He bestows upon us the role of stewards, which means we are to watch over and manage what belongs to God. You are a steward of the Lord. With that comes one of the greatest challenges linked to our perception of the world: OWNERSHIP.

Everything belongs to God. A "this is mine" mindset will destroy your ability to act as a steward. Since the job of a steward is to tend someone else's possessions, the quickest way to ruin your ability to effectively manage what God has given you is to start thinking that you are the actual owner. Some people treat other people's things better than they treat their own, because they know they are responsible to others when using or looking out for those things. When you have an ownership mentality, you start handling His belongings as if you are not accountable to Him for how you use them.

Have you ever used the argument, "I work hard for my money; I'm not just going to give it away" to justify holding back what you have? God has entrusted you with the privileged role of steward, but if you are stingy with what He has given you, why would He give you more? He has authority over government, and by extension, over all of the money in the world. He controls all of creation and keeps everything in motion, so the fact that you can even earn money is through His grace. Every penny you receive has come through the hands of the Lord, and still more, He has asked you to represent Him through each word, action, and deed—including how you handle your possessions.

What you need to do is remind yourself that your money is first and foremost His money. From this mindset, you can be truly grateful for what He allows you to have, however little or much, and you can begin to take on proper stewardship of that money. You do not give God a fraction of what is yours, but rather you consider how you should spend His money to handle your necessities, then give the rest back to Him.

All this time, you have really been living on His money. Only the enemy is glad when you believe that what you have is your own and belongs primarily to you. There is only one thing you truly own and can keep with you through everything: your soul. Everything else you have right now is given into your stewardship. You will not keep it—but God will judge you based on how you use it. Don't get stuck in the secular mindset of ownership. Once you learn how to behave as a trustworthy steward, then God will be able to use you for great things.

The Origin of Tithing

Tithing is popularly believed to have started with Abraham paying tithes to Melchizedek, but it has a history reaching back further than even that. In the Garden of Eden, God told Adam, *"Of every tree of the garden thou mayest freely eat: But of the tree of the knowledge of good and evil, thou shalt not eat of it"* (Genesis 2:16b–17a). God expected Adam to be willing to surrender something fully unto God, through obedience and acknowledgement of God's sovereignty.

God didn't put a gate around the tree or put a fire around it to keep Adam and Eve out, but rather He left it in their domain, under their care, for them to honor Him by surrendering their ability to partake of it. He gave them a crucial charge: "Sanctify this unto Me out of all you have." When they refused to follow that one command, they lost everything they had and were thrown out of their perfect home. They lost access to more than just Eden: they lost their personal connection to the Lord and His near presence, which was what resulted in the death He warned them against.

As you study the Scriptures, you will see that God gives everything, and requires us to give everything back to serve Him. He expects us to sanctify unto Him what He gives us—our time, our talent, our earthly goods, and our lives. The One who gave us everything waits for us to give back in turn.

Your talents are not something you learn how to do through your own agenda, but something innate, natural, that you foster through your life. God graced you with talent, so you are required to return it to Him through service. The church does not only need a tithe of money—that is only a fraction of what God has blessed you with in this life. Worldwide, local churches struggle because the skilled don't have the spirit of service, and the ones who wish to serve are not equipped with all the necessary skills. Building a heart of service in the skilled and maintaining the same heart in the unskilled is a difficulty the church would not have to face if only we would all dedicate ourselves to God.

God wants you, not only your pocketbook. He seeks you, specifically, individually, and He is ready to help you use all you possess through Him to further the glory of the Kingdom. Still, this is not an excuse to hold onto your money: when you lay it down for the service of God, you are upholding the physical sanctuary you attend and sustaining the ministries you support. Whenever God moves in those places, then you will have your small part in that movement too, whether you are present or absent. When you pay your tithe and give your offerings, you humble yourself and sow the seeds for present and future work.

Understanding the Tithe

It is one thing to go to a lawyer only when a time of need catches up to you, but quite another to have a lawyer on retainer. When you have a lawyer on retainer, you pay a regular sum to him so that whenever legal issues arise, you can call on him for help. At any time, he will be available to you because you have paid him to be on retainer.

In the same way, God in times past had an arrangement with His people: if they would render to Him the annual offering, the first fruits, then He would give them aid and increase. He wanted them to pay the honorarium, and then He would give to them in abundance from that investment every time they reached out to Him.

Leviticus, an oft-overlooked book, describes the system of tithing based on Mosaic law:

> And all the tithe of the land, whether of the seed of the land, or of the fruit of the tree, is the Lord's: it is holy unto the Lord. And if a man will at all redeem ought of his tithes, he shall add thereto the fifth part thereof. And concerning the tithe of the herd, or of the flock, even of whatsoever passeth under the rod, the tenth shall be holy unto the Lord. He shall not search whether it be good or bad, neither shall he change it: and if he change it at all, then both it and the change thereof shall be holy; it shall not be redeemed (Leviticus 27:30–33).

The tenth shall be holy unto the Lord—the minimum God decreed. The tithe, in its most basic form, is a tenth of everything we have. Whether a tenth of one dollar or a tenth of one million dollars, the percentage remains the same. Some people don't mind tithing in poverty, since the amount given over does not seem excessive, but when they make more, then they want to manipulate matters so they can keep back everything they can, because they feel that it is what they earned, and they want to control it.

"Thou shalt truly tithe all the increase of thy seed, that the field bringeth forth year by year" (Deuteronomy 14:22). God does not want us to withhold our blessings, since they came from Him initially, and He has the power to increase them still more when we prove faithful to His decrees. The annual tithe was not meant to rob or deprive His people, but to help them and to bring glory to God and to them.

> *Will a man rob God? Yet ye have robbed Me. But ye say, 'Wherein have we robbed Thee?' In tithes and offerings. Ye are cursed with a curse: for ye have robbed Me, even this whole nation. Bring ye all the tithes into the storehouse, that there may be meat in Mine house, and prove Me now herewith, saith the Lord of hosts, if I will not open you the windows of heaven, and pour you out a blessing, that there shall not be room enough to receive it. And I will rebuke the devourer for your sakes, and he shall not destroy the fruits of your ground; neither shall your vine cast her fruit before the time in the field, saith the Lord of hosts. And all nations shall call you blessed: for ye shall be a delightsome land, saith the Lord of hosts.* (Malachi 3:8–12).

God repeatedly challenged His people to test Him on the promises He made to them, because He always intended to fulfill them. He wanted to bless His people, and He used the tithe as one of the methods of testing their obedience before rewarding them.

"Bring ye"—this is how you cancel a curse and invoke the blessings of God instead. Malachi also spoke also of "all the tithes," instead of only one, or even several, handed over to the Lord. You are meant to bring all your tithes to the house of God; you cannot simply dedicate some money to a secular charity or similar place and expect that to serve God in the same way as a tithe devoted directly to Him.

Most importantly of all, however, Jesus uncovers the heart of tithing, *"Woe unto you, scribes and Pharisees, hypocrites! for ye pay tithe of mint and anise and cumin, and have omitted the weightier matters of the law, judgment, mercy, and faith: these ought ye to have done, and not to leave the other undone"* (Matthew 23:23). He made it evident that simply taking a tenth of everything, down to the smallest of things, is not the true intent of God. He does indeed want us to tithe—"not to leave the other undone"—but He expects it to come from a heart of love and faith. Do not believe anyone who tells you that you do not have to tithe in the dispensation of grace, or that you can just give free-will offerings or donations to God and He will be satisfied. He judges the hearts of men first, then He acknowledges their outward actions.

Giving only as the Lord prospers you is not enough. Tithes and offerings are both necessary for proper worship and stewardship in all seasons of life. Whatever your conscience encourages you to give, give unto the Lord. You must take care not to rob the Lord your God. Instead, you must find ways to express your love and appreciation for what He has given and will give.

The Annual Tithe and the Tithe of Every Increase

As addressed in Deuteronomy 14:22, God says that every increase, or profit, requires tithing. For you, that is every check, every blessing, every promotion, every raise, every business deal—whatever you receive.

You might find yourself in a situation, like attending college, where you need to take out a loan to pay for school. That is not an increase, because you have to pay it back with interest, and it is only covering your immediate needs. However, if you get a loan for $15,000, but the school only requires $10,000, then $5,000 of that is an increase, because it was not immediately spent, but rather increased the money you had on hand. Likewise, you can tithe your refunds, because they increased you in the moment.

There is also the tithe of the increase of the increase, otherwise known as the first fruits offering. Let us say you make $24,000 a year ($2,000 a month). Roughly every two weeks, you would then make $1,000.

If you received a double in salary ($48,000 per year, $4,000 per month), then you would increase from $1,000 to $2,000 every two weeks. The first increase belongs to God: the first extra $1,000 is a proper offering to give as a one-time tithe for a one-time increase.

The annual tithe is like first fruits also, since it is what you set aside at the beginning of the year from what God has blessed you with, and you will in turn give back to Him. Annual, or yearly, tithing is meant to function as steady support for God's ministry. A three-year tithe was part of the Mosaic law and served an important purpose:

> *At the end of three years thou shalt bring forth all the tithe of thine increase the same year, and shalt lay it up within thy gates: And the Levite (because he hath no part nor inheritance with thee), and the stranger, and the fatherless, and the widow, which are within thy gates, shall come, and shall eat and be satisfied; that the Lord thy God may bless thee in all the work of thine hand which thou doest* (Deuteronomy 14:28–29).

15

Those who could not fend for themselves or work in a way that would give them a secure salary were provided for through this tithe. The priests were included because they and their family, the Levites, did not get an inheritance in the land, and they were dedicated to serving the Lord and helping the people. Because they were set apart to serve God and His house, God made sure to provide for them through the rest of His people. In the same way, we should be willing to support with our money those who dedicate their lives to the ministry of God—not the ministry of religion, but the true and whole-hearted works of God.

Those who preach the Gospel should live off the Gospel. They should not be forced to work a secular career also. God looked out for His priests before, and we should continue in that work today, so that those who care for God's people can give their full time to the maintenance and prayer for the church and ministry of God.

Before, God set aside tithes specifically for the care of His priests, to ensure that they could follow Him instead of the world. He even saw to their food: they were allowed to eat whatever the fire did not consume of the offerings. Through this, the priests' food, living arrangements, clothes, and everything else necessary for life were to come from the people.

The gold and the silver in Solomon's temple, too, came from the people. Because of this, the adornment of the temple and the priests represented the people and reflected their interest in and commitment to God.

Today, we have lost sight of that union with the endeavors of our local churches. The enemy wars against us, embellishing the idea of personal ownership and detracting from the idea of communal ministry. We are led to believe that when we finish tithing, we will have lost something instead of having gained something.

When you fully obey God in surrender, He makes what is His available to you. You can empty out all that is required of you and more, and He is able to keep you. You only need to test Him to find He is faithful.

Offerings beyond the Tithe

Like Malachi clarifies by saying *"in tithes and offerings,"* God does not only look for tithes from us. Even a quick preview of the Old Testament shows that there were numerous types of offerings given to the Lord, but some were not mandatory: the peace offerings, the grain and drink offerings, and the burnt offerings. Why, you might ask, did the people give so much above and beyond the bare minimum required of them? Voluntary offerings express your gratitude, appreciation, and love for God. You owe tithes, but giving of what you are allowed to keep back is a free-will expression of worship.

In our modern times, we have offerings for things like pastor appreciation. The point of this is for you to show your pastor that you appreciate how he serves the whole congregation, not only how he serves you. Giving to such an offering is about gratitude. If you feel stressed, obligated, or put upon, then you should not give your money, because the amount of money brought in is not the point.

You should never allow yourself to feel coerced into giving an offering—you should give out of love and nothing else. If you appreciate and value your church, then such offerings are not a headache or a chore: you simply feel glad to bless your church and support it, and you fulfill the role assigned to voluntary offerings.

Benefits of Giving

As stated before, the end result of tithes and offerings is not just that you give something: you receive in turn. If you are willing to humble yourself in obedience of stewardship, then God will bless you with excess, now or in future, in ways imaginable and unimaginable.

"Give, and it shall be given unto you; good measure, pressed down, and shaken together, and running over, shall men give into your bosom. For with the same measure that ye mete withal it shall be measured to you again" (Luke 6:38). God, in His good time, justly rewards those who follow Him. He longs to bless His people. When you give tithes and offerings, God works through you and for you, because you are following His commands and desires.

Offerings can make a world of difference in your life. Hearts could soften towards you, financial support could come, and most importantly, God will be pleased with you. Giving unto God provides you with untold benefits and blessings, so you must never forget the good that will return to you. God is able to open the windows of heaven and cause blessings to be poured out on you; He is able to turn the hearts of men toward you and encourage men to bless you, also.

In the days of Noah, God showed another facet of this truth. As Genesis 6:9 tells us, "Noah was a just man and perfect in his generations, and Noah walked with God." Because he followed God, he was spared from the terrible judgment God unleashed on the earth. However, God not only spared Noah and his family because of Noah's obedience and just heart, but gave to him in abundance: everything in the restored world was at Noah's disposal for food and living. After a season of destruction, Noah saw God replenish the earth and restore the good things therein. Not only did Noah escape with his life, but he received manifold blessings from the renewed world.

God will replenish everything that is destroyed, even that which is destroyed by His great army. Like Jesus told Martha, He is "the resurrection and the life" (John 11:25). God has the power to restore everything lost. If something is torn down, He can build it up; if people destroy something, He can raise it up again; if you are beaten down, He can pick you up again, too.

Noah received the promise of the rainbow. Although in recent times the world has tried to demean it as a symbol for gay rights, the rainbow is in fact what God gave as the sign of the enduring covenant that God would not again destroy all life on earth by water, no matter how far wickedness spread. Instead, He would wait for the very end of the world to bring about a final judgment. Every time it rains, God establishes His promise again in our minds with the rainbow He created: "I am a keeper of My promises."

Now, we have a still greater promise, that of Jesus Christ, offering us eternity with Him in the richness and security of heaven, if only we obey Him now in love and faith.

The Harvest after Seed Time

With the flood, God had washed the earth clean. It seemed hopelessly destroyed, but He had merely bathed it in water to purify it for a fresh start, and He promised He would not drastically alter creation again in such a manner. *While the earth remaineth, seedtime and harvest, and cold and heat, and summer and winter, and day and night shall not cease"* (Genesis 8:22). We can count on God preserving the natural world as He has decreed, and we should likewise count on Him to carry out the decrees He has made to us.

God promised to bless the harvests of His people if they obeyed Him. Few of us now are looking for a literal harvest, but we can hand over other financial efforts to the Lord. You can use your money as a seed now. If you ask for God's leading in investment, He can bring a return to bless you. Some people wish they had some seed in Microsoft, Home Depot, Wal-Mart, or

QuikTrip, but you don't need to focus on what already looks successful. If you surrender your income to the Lord and act as His faithful steward, even investing in a small way is good: God will bring about the increase He is ready for you to have. Sow your seed with the anointing of the Spirit, and there is no chance of real loss; the earth will always produce after that which is put in it.

When you come across a situation where you can sow your seed into the ground where it is needed, this is called benevolence. Sometimes you do not invest in some marketable venue, but rather in someone or something that God calls you to give your money to for His purposes. Sometimes, even, it seems as if you are giving money where there is no apparent need. In such cases you are surrendering your money to use as a seed for whatever God has purposed. Giving in benevolence is fulfilling a need you can see, but when you sow a seed when you cannot see a need, you command the earth to receive it, multiply it, and return it.

If you give one hundred dollars and the Holy Ghost tells you to give eighty more, do not hesitate, even if you will have nothing left afterward. Even if everything God gave you initially is gone, God does not forget. You are a carrier of His glory, and in your need, He can shine brightest. He gave you the $180, but He will multiply it later, whether in an increase of money, from $180 to $18,000, or something else. Don't ever slip into the mindset of ownership by saying, "God, I passed the test, so this increase is now mine." Regardless of how much you shout, dance, speak in tongues, or display other expressions of spirituality, if you cannot tithe your salary as it becomes larger, then God's place has not be hallowed in your life.

God tests you first in the little things to see if He can test you with the great ones. He wants to prove He can trust you in a small way before He trusts you with unlimited resources. The enemy does not want you to have God's infinite resources, spiritual or of this world, because once you access all that God has for you, you become a powerful steward of the Lord.

The Challenges of Giving

Hopefully, you already give. You put your gain back in His hand, dropping it into the bucket or slipping it into the envelope, whenever you are called to give. But what's the point in bringing tithe, offering, and seed when you are comfortable and secure in what you already have, or, perhaps, when you are struggling to get by? Why do you constantly pour money into the church? The Bible says it should be done, but why, if God already has all the resources He needs, does your money count?

The benefit of giving your money has nothing to do with the money itself; you are to practice being faithful to God and you are allowed the chance to see Him be faithful in turn. You express your love by giving up what the world says will benefit you here and now. God has called you to be holy, and the value of sowing your money as seeds for Him shows that you will not withhold your temporal benefits from Him. You recognize that God has given you the job you have—your resume didn't do it, your name didn't do it, your connections didn't do it—and He is in control of your future income. His favor is worth more to you than a check.

Oftentimes, little salaries are not the problem in giving to God; rather, abundance makes it difficult. Just because you can stop wearing Payless shoes doesn't mean you're special now and no longer need God's provision. He made you a steward, and stewardship means you must be prepared to give an account at any moment and to hand over whatever is requested of you, since it does not belong to you.

Recently at a conference, I had on a tie that I had only worn twice in the years I'd had it, because it was a special tie. Someone walked up to me and complimented me on that tie. The first time,

I said thank you and tried to move on, but the person repeated it again. That time, I felt the Holy Ghost prompt me to give up the tie. I tried to avoid the nudge, saying that I liked the tie, it was one of my good ones, but He objected. He recalled to my mind that I was not an owner, but a steward, so I took off the tie and gave it up. Before I left the conference, however, I found nine additional ties placed on my back seat.

Whenever God takes anything from you, whatever you hand over at His command, even the most insignificant, material things, God will see that you are provided for and brought under His blessing. You must give because His honor is the one thing of value that you have to gain. His glory is everything, in the present and in the future, and whatever stands in the way of His glory must go.

If you have a house, make sure something returns to the service of God from your house, because you want Him to have a place in your home, like He has a place in your income. Sanctify Him in everything you have. You do not need to fear giving, because God has already given you everything you need, freely and in love.

You can show your love for Him by doing what He requires. He knows what you owe others, He knows every bill you have, He knows what necessities you have to buy, but He still asks for you to surrender to Him. Your perspective might still be skewed, because you see that you worked long hours to earn your paycheck, but consider: Who kept you safe through the night so you could wake? Who kept the life in your body? Who gave you the strength to continue working? Who helped you keep your job in a struggling economy?

If you lose your job, if you don't get that paycheck, there is still no cause for alarm, because God is in control of your lack as much as He is in control of your abundance. Even with the same bills and needs, He can provide. When you cannot work, God is taking care of you. You may even find, when you get another job and see the change, that when you were unemployed you still had money to cover every need and more, which is no longer supplied now that you can work.

God does not require you to return to Him all that He gives you, since He gives to you freely and lets you use what He has bestowed. Still, He trusts that you will acknowledge Him with the tithe He is due. Ten percent is enough to show the Lord that you will love and obey Him, but He is ready to do so much more for you than what you do for Him. He knows the value of what you have, but He wants to do exceedingly, abundantly above anything you can ask or think, so He encourages you to act on faith in Him so He can bless you.

You can miss out on many miraculous experiences when you defy the prompting of the Holy Spirit. If God calls you to surrender two hundred, but you keep it back because you need it for a bill, then He cannot show you the great works He has in mind, nor reward you for your obedient service. He tugs at your heart; He leaves you to decide if you will give unto Him.

The flesh often fights back when He calls for us to act in His will, but honoring God in our giving grants us access to the realm of the unlimited. We must nurture the giving spirit in this nation, to honor God and receive His blessings, or else we will bring about the same displeasure God described through Malachi. If we do not want to rob God, we need to look beyond our lack of immediate needs and look to the glory of God and the blessings He wants to provide. According to Him, the only way He can give unlimited blessings to us is for us to hallow Him in all of our areas of interest. To bring His blessing and reflect His glory, you must give without stint or grumbling. Honor God with your money in obedient stewardship, and He will honor you.

2 The Manifestation of Sons

"For the earnest expectation of the creature waiteth for the manifestation of the sons of God" (Romans 8:19). God has positioned each of us in our lives and in our individual circumstances so that He can reveal Himself in us. We have the designated privilege of carrying the revelation of God fitted to where we are in our walk with Him and in our lives.

You, as a glory carrier, bear the revelation of God that is congruous with who you are designed to be and where you are designed to be. You may not be in a desirable place, but God has allowed you to be there for an express purpose. He can use you and where you are to reveal Himself to other people who are in the same place, or to reveal Himself more fully to you. You will not be subjected to an unappealing place because you are useless or because of your history. Your present is not your punishment: it is your assignment, based on what God has given you to do, soon to be revealed.

God often sends His best to the worst situations. If you are in a horrible place, know that He is ready to use you in mighty ways as soon as you are ready to serve Him where you are. You can shine wherever you are, and the difficulties surrounding you can be taken in hand by His power to produce the results He needs.

If you study the first chapter of Colossians, you will realize that the great mystery spoken of there is the glory of God reaching not only Abraham's descendants, but everyone who will turn to Him. When you are filled with the glory through Christ, you are responsible for letting it shine, unfiltered, out of you. You are not responsible to reveal Jesus Christ to the whole earthly realm: you are only responsible for the revelation of where you are set and where you are sent. People make the mistake of assuming they have to travel to reveal their faith, but if every Christian would simply preach the Gospel where they already live, the world would be reached as a matter of course by those God has placed all over the world for His work. We prefer the idea of preaching across the globe, not in our own backyards. Saving Asia seems easier than saving our neighborhood.

God has a record of setting changed people in unchanged places. You don't have to go far. God says, "I am in you. I will strengthen you for where I have you." You don't have to change your address or get on a plane to be used by God. That is the mindset of someone who does not know the will of God.

The challenge of revealing God where you are is that people generally know you well, and they know who you used to be. You have to act in a new, consistent way to reflect the glory now in you. Often, we are stuck being babes, mere children of God, instead of transitioning fully into sons of God.

When we remain children of God (not in age, but in mentality) and keep that mindset, we will not manifest the full privilege of sonship, which is part of the revelation of who He is in us.

God does not remain aloof in heaven. He is revealing Himself through the glory and the Holy Spirit He has put in us. We are indeed glory carriers! Heaven does not contain all of the glory of God, because He has invested His glory in every one of His children.

> *He was in the world, and the world was made by Him, and the world knew Him not. He came unto His own, and His own received Him not. But as many as received Him, to them gave He power to become the sons of God, even to them that believe on His name* (John 1:10–12).

Here we can plainly see that the world was made by Him. Nothing was made that was not made by Him. What's more? He was in the world He had made, but nobody in the world knew Him.

27

In other words, everybody was enjoying the benefits of His labor, but nobody took the time to be in an acknowledging, humble relationship with Him so that they could recognize Him. If you live like that, if you deny a relevant Jesus, then you are living in the world that He made while at the same time rejecting Him.

You should know, also, that in verse twelve, the Greek word used for "sons" is "teknon," meaning "children." The text is saying that during rebirth, you become born again and thus become a child of God (a *teknon*), but that does not mean you instantaneously become a son of God. Many people think that because they are saved, they are sons. Not quite. Initially, you're a *teknon*, a child of God. To be a son of God, you have to go a little further.

Children of God

Do all things without murmurings and disputings: that ye may be blameless and harmless, the sons of God, without rebuke, in the midst of a crooked and perverse nation, among whom ye shine as lights in the world (Philippians 2:14–15).

God calls us to separate ourselves from the disobedient and worldly to show our relationship with Him in righteousness. This text again uses *teknon*, which stresses how you are called to be children of purity in the presence of wickedness. Even though the unbelievers outnumber you, they are not greater than you, because *"greater is He that is in you, than he that is in the world"* (1 John 4:4b).

Throughout the Bible, you will find examples of how the sheer number of those in opposition or those in defense does not matter. Jericho fell, the Assyrians were turned back, and the Egyptians were confounded in their own country. When God raised Gideon to free Israel, the army of 300,000 he brought together was too much: God whittled it down over and over again until only three hundred Israelites remained, then He sent them off to win the war against an enemy that far exceeded their own number. He did all of that to prove His sovereignty over every circumstance. No human measures can win the day without His consent, and no single set of hands can fail if He has decreed success. You never have to be intimidated by the overwhelming presence of wickedness and wicked people.

You never have to give in to what they're doing, what they're saying, or how they're behaving. Such steadfastness in character is how people can distinguish the children of God from the rest, because their godly behavior shows that they are born again, set apart.

The reason we compromise in challenging settings is that we don't believe in the power that dwells in us. We start to wonder if the prince of the world has the real power; and if perhaps we would be better off if we followed everyone else. We feel like we might lose something if we don't at least look like them, but as 2 Corinthians 6:17 states, *"...come out from among them, and be ye separate, saith the Lord."* That does not mean we have to move away from those in the world or refrain from engaging them, but rather that we are to be distinctly different as we live around them.

You have the command to be different when you are a child of God. You don't have to try to fit in with the trends, match your wardrobe to the fashions, or enjoy drinks and drugs with your peers. You're distinguished—you've become a little more special than you were before, because you've been brought into God's spiritual family.

Once you're born again, your life is drastically altered, even if you cannot see any change in your physical form compared to others, or your intelligence compared to others, or anything else. It is much like an adult and a teenager. While in the teen years, the person is underage, but once he reaches adulthood, he has grown beyond youth and can never return. He can say to other teens, "What I now am, you can be, too. What you are, I can never be again." Although an adult cannot go back in time to be younger, but when you are born again, you can choose to go back to a less mature time of life by rejecting God. You can decide to be as the world is, or you can choose to follow God in maturity. Those of the world are free to choose God over their lifestyles and opinions, too, but they must go through the process of spiritual rebirth.

I have chosen to be a child of God, even though I live in a perverse nation. I'm a child of God amongst wicked people, working on my job where so many ignorant, heathen individuals dislike me, but I have in me One who is greater than they (See 1 John 4:4). If they fire me, my Heavenly Father will see that I am provided for, and I will never have to stoop to what they require or desire. First and foremost, I am a child of God, and I will follow Him.

1 John 3:1–2 says:

Behold, what manner of love the Father hath bestowed upon us, that we should be called the sons of God: therefore the world knoweth us not, because it knew Him not. Beloved, now are we the sons of God, and it doth not yet appear what we shall be: but we know that, when He shall appear, we shall be like Him; for we shall see Him as He is.

Again, the text uses the word *teknon*. As children of God, we hold the position of the new birth, born of the Spirit into the family of God. The verse says it does not yet appear what we shall be, and that is because we have not yet begun to be. We have just come into that position. When born again, you begin again. From there, you proceed towards sonship. You are saved, but you're still not wholly transformed into the image of Christ: you have to work towards the completion God has for you. You are to pursue the salvation of your soul "with fear and trembling" (See Philippians 2:12), not with a one-time act. To be a true son of God requires spiritual rebirth and a new way of life.

You are not a child of God just because you acknowledge God. People who claim to be a child of God first need to consider whether they are born again. You are not by your first birth, the physical birth, a child of God. Just because you are here and want to give credit to God for helping you once in a while doesn't mean you are an actual child of God. If you have not been born again by the Spirit, if your spirit has not been changed by the blood of Christ and by the indwelling of the Holy Spirit, then you are not even a *teknon*. You are not saved if you have not been born again, because you are not a part of the kingdom. Just because you join a church doesn't mean you're born again. You have to go through rebirth through the Spirit. Attending church doesn't make you saved any more than wearing glasses makes you see: if you don't have the right prescription for glasses, they won't help you see any better. Likewise, you have to enter the church with the right heart, enabled to see and hear by the transformation of salvation, or else it does not help you.

When we are born again, we receive a new Father. *"For as many as are led by the Spirit of God, they are the sons of God. For ye have not received the spirit of bondage again to fear; but ye have received the Spirit of adoption, whereby we cry, 'Abba, Father'"* (Romans 8:14–15). Before God adopted us, our father was the one who controls the wicked of the world: satan, who entices you to serve him by first serving yourself. All he wants for you is to get you to fall like he did. Furthermore, satan's fall came from his desire to be equal with God; he wanted to follow his own rules, live his own way, and receive glory for himself. That same desire is how Satan ensnares so many of the world—he pushes us

31

to want the same thing he did, to live our lives the way we see fit instead of how God wants.

When we reject the temptation and accept Jesus as Lord, then we can call out to God the Father as our own Father. As we reaffirm His fatherhood over us, He encourages us to, instead of living our lives, live His life in us, because He has brought us back to life spiritually through His power. He gives us each the choice to live either His life or ours, and our actions will show our answer to His offer.

Living your own way is not all it's cracked up to be. Living your own life will only get you cheap, quick imitations that do not ultimately satisfy. Everything God causes you to desire comes out of His life, not yours. Everything God promises us is brought about only when we are living the life He has for us. You will never be fulfilled while you aren't living to show the results of the glory He has placed in you. Satisfaction, authentic happiness, and fulfillment will never be yours if you are bent on pursuing your life. You have to go after His instead:

> Then said Jesus unto His disciples, 'If any man will come after Me, let him deny himself, and take up his cross, and follow Me. For whosoever will save his life shall lose it: and whosoever will lose his life for My sake shall find it. For what is a man profited, if he shall gain the whole world, and lose his own soul? or what shall a man give in exchange for his soul? For the Son of Man shall come in the glory of His Father with His angels; and then He shall reward every man according to his works (Matthew 16:24–27).

To successfully do as Jesus commands, learn to live the prayer from Matthew 6:10, *"Thy kingdom come, Thy will be done, in earth as it is in heaven."* We all need to seek first the Kingdom of God and to pursue His righteousness, at whatever cost.

Everything will be added to us if we pursue His life (See Matthew 6:33), but the enemy will try every trick to keep us from that blessing. Our adversary will give us little trinkets and fleeting pleasures to make it seem like we are getting the equivalent to God's promises, but it is all a gimmick to keep us miserable and dead in the spirit. The devil can give you a house, but he can't give you a home. He can give you a mattress, but he can't give you rest. He can give you all kinds of objects, but he can't give you life. Jesus, on the other hand, said, *"I am come that they might have life, and that they might have it more abundantly"* (John 10:10b).

By the Holy Spirit, we are given new life. *"For ye have not received the spirit of bondage again to fear; but ye have received the Spirit of adoption"* (Romans 8:15). The Spirit seals us unto the day of redemption, proving that we have left behind the old, the spirit of the world, and have become children of God. *"The Spirit itself beareth witness with our spirit, that we are the children of God"* (Romans 8:16). The Spirit helps show our spirits that we are *teknon*, that we have entered a new family that will radically change how we live.

Have you recognized the difference between the Holy Spirit and your spirit? Not everything in your spirit is of the Holy Spirit. The way your spirit becomes a reflection of the Holy Spirit is by consistency in worship, prayer, and service. Then will the Holy Spirit be poured all the more abundantly into you to transform you into the image of Christ. This is never a single event in your life, but a constant thing.

If you miss worship in your daily consecration, your spirit lacks what it needs and becomes more self-centered. You become untrustworthy. If you do not actively seek God, you have stayed away from your assigned place too long.

33

"And if children, then heirs; heirs of God, and joint-heirs with Christ; if so be that we suffer with Him, that we may be also glorified together" (Romans 8:17). As children of God, we have something to inherit. We are more than simply heirs to a fortune or a title—we are heirs of God and joint-heirs with Christ. Everything Jesus is to receive, you will receive in heirship. He is the model of the inheritance, the firstborn of many brethren (See Romans 8:29). If Christ conquered, so shall we when we are joined to Him. If He overcame, we shall likewise overcome. What He suffers, we suffer, and through such suffering we come to glory.

Your suffering is limited to what Christ suffered. If what you are suffering falls outside of that, release the problem from your life and let God take care of the rest. Jesus was tempted in all ways, but nothing got Him. You likewise are empowered to escape temptation. We suffer with Him so that we may be glorified together. He has already ascended and received the glory of the Father, so we too can receive the glory because He has sent the Spirit back to us, that we shall be glory carriers for Him.

All of the promises of God are in Christ, and thus they are only in you if you are in Christ. Not being in Christ eliminates you from everything of God. So, who is Christ exactly? Let us break this down, to understand Christ, the "Christos," the "Anointed One."

> *In the beginning was the Word, and the Word was with God, and the Word was God. The same was in the beginning with God. All things were made by Him; and without Him was not anything made that was made. In Him was life; and the life was the light of men. ... And the Word was made flesh, and dwelt among us, (and we beheld His glory, the glory as of the only begotten of the Father), full of grace and truth* (John 1:1–4, 14).

When He dwelt amongst us, what was His name? Jesus the Messiah, or in Greek, "the Christ." He said that He is the Word, the way, the truth, and the life. If you live outside of Jesus, you are disqualified. You are far from everything God has to offer. When you disregard any part of the Word, you disregard Jesus, because all of it is the revelation of Jesus Christ.

The Word is what reveals Christ to us. Not movies, not music, not art. If you depend on gospel music to reveal Christ to you, you're not going to get to know Him. If you depend on preaching alone, you're not going to get to know Him. You have to know the Word, personally and fully.

The Word is the manifestation of Jesus Christ in our time. When you read watered down or paraphrased versions, you lose parts of the revelation, because some translators' print versions leave out words, phrases, sentences, even whole sections, and in reading only those, you become a pursuer of ease, not of holiness.

We cannot pursue ease instead of Christ. No easy translation will give you a free pass from studying the Word in its fullness. If you read the CliffsNotes on Shakespeare, you're not going to get the complete, authentic experience. You have to go to the original to really learn. The same is especially true of the Bible. Get as close as you can to the authentic experience, and you will draw closer to Jesus and His truth.

The Emerging Glory

"For I reckon that the sufferings of this present time are not worthy to be compared with the glory which shall be revealed in us" (Romans 8:18). In this verse, Paul puts us in the proper perspective in relation to being joint-heirs. Suffering is one of the things included in joint-heirship. He reckons—assesses, concludes—that the sufferings that were happening currently when he wrote to the Church could not compare with the glory that

God would reveal within them through those trials. The same is true of all of us who are born again.

Because you are a glory carrier, your suffering is bound up in the revelation of glory, not for you, but for Him in whatever place He has put you and whomever He has put around you. You are to reflect glory back on the Savior and help Him in that work as much as He will allow you. Your suffering is for the increase of glory, and your trials could give you the tools you need to help someone come to saving grace. Through your struggle, someone could become more than a conqueror. Because of this, it is a privilege as a glory carrier to pass through struggles and sufferings, so that you can have the key to help someone else who would otherwise have died before they made it. Some things you go through, some things you've been through, are because you are being prepared to help other people, who would have instead given in to despair and jumped off a bridge, sliced their wrists, or blown their heads off because of their inability to save themselves. You could have done the same, but that which is greater than the world prevented you. Once you conquer in certain areas, you are equipped to help deliver others and cause the change God intends to carry out in the "lost" of the world.

Often, I sit in my office and counsel people, and while I talk with and listen to them, I can start to relate my experiences to what they're going through. I have concluded that God made me pass through what has happened in my life because of the people who come to me now. I went through hell so I could snatch people out of it. God trusted me with the difficulties I faced because He knew that, like Job, I would not curse Him and die because of trials. He has likewise assessed you, and He only leads you through what you can handle. He knows you have the ability to face your trials for His glory, and He is waiting to bless you, even though He will not cut the experience short before you learn everything you need to from it, even when you are tired or angry or crying. When you try to avoid your trial, He pulls you back because He has fully pre-qualified you not just for the suffering, but for the miracle.

Your difficulties may be extreme. If I passed through what you experience, perhaps I would end up cursing, or doing any number of impatient, irreverent things. I was not pre-qualified to go through what you're going through; I can only pray that you can stand what I cannot. I am given my own trials that I am qualified to take, because the support God has given me is sufficient for that, and He has given the same to you. What we experience now is not worthy to be compared to what we're coming to, so we can keep our eyes turned forward and remember that God is with us every step of the way.

"For as many as are led by the Spirit of God, they are the sons of God" (Romans 8:14). Here, we have a hint at what being a son of God is: it means we are led by God, governed by something greater than what is in our own minds and wills. Sonship is related to conduct, the evidence of the dignity of your relationship with God and your likeness to His character. Just as you can tell who a child's parents are by what the child looks like and how he acts, the world can tell who your spiritual father is by how you behave. Conduct determines whose son you are just as rebirth determines the children of God. I don't want to just be a child of God. I want to be a son.

Sonship is not a position but a demonstration. I am a son because of how I carry myself and show forth the glory that I carry inside. There is always an option at every moment to either show forth glory or show forth self-will. You have the glory of God because you're His child, but in demonstrating the glory of God you show that you are His son.

"For the earnest expectation of the creature waiteth for the manifestation of the sons of God" (Romans 8:19). The people who have been placed in your life are looking for the manifestation of

sons, not of children. They look for those who would demonstrate glory, not merely bury it deep inside.

I don't want to carry what I can't show forth. Who wants to be pregnant and never bring the child into the world? In the same way, what we have in us is meant to be brought into a tangible, radiant form in this world. God wants to transform our mindset from children of God, who are positional inheritors, to the mindset of sons of God, who work with the Spirit through their salvation.

There are certain things the other glory carriers around you can do that you can't because you carry an individual revelation of glory. You cannot judge your salvation by the weaker or stronger brothers near you. You have to move and grow by the leading of the Spirit within you to be a fully-formed son of God. What the people around you in church learn from a sermon will not be precisely what you learn, because of the different revelations God can give through the same words and situations. You might feel confused when you hear other people talking about their revelation because that was not what you received, but it is merely because their glory is different than yours. God does not reveal His total self to any one person. No, He reveals that which is necessary to manifest the deposit that He has placed in you.

As a result, the world waits on your help. They're waiting for you because you're equipped to help in a way no one else is. There are people waiting who you are assigned to help with the glory placed in you. While you waste your time on social media, pretending to connect with the world through Facebook or Twitter or some other outlet, you miss the chance to show forth your glory to those nearest to you.

They are waiting for the manifestation of the son in you, not the child. Believers all have the identity of the *teknon*, but more of us need to behave as sons. We need the conduct not just in church, but out of it: in the marketplace, in the home, in the neighborhood, in the workforce, in the gym, everywhere. We need to comport ourselves as sons.

They're waiting on you. They're not waiting on a quick wit, a brash attitude, or a sharp tongue—they're waiting on your willingness to comport yourself according to the revelation of God in you. They're waiting to see the glory you carry. You cannot carry anyone else's glory; you have to figure out who He is yourself and show that, grow in that.

You are in a situation you are qualified for, to do what you do, give what you give, and sacrifice what you sacrifice as a son. Your conduct demonstrates your sonship, not your position as a child. You are meant to show the world who He is and what you really are through Him. Your actions should only show the appropriate behavior for sons. Praise God like a son, dress like a son, speak like a son. Glorying in things of this world, dressing for the attention of this world, or speaking like everyone else in the world proves through your conduct that you are not His son.

You can identify those of the world by their reaction to your following the Father. What the rest of the world considers a chore or a burden is your privilege as a son. The world will never understand, because you are a son and they are not.

Faith will take you far beyond the perspective held by the world. The enemy wants to bring you back down to the warped reality of the sin nature, but you have to shed that and assume the conduct of a son. As a glory carrier, you have a beauty like the Ark of the Covenant. Not only are you as beautiful, but you are as detailed. The mercy seat and the law of God rest in you. When you enter someone's house, your presence will bless that house and those you come in contact with, as long as you are a son of God. You contain that which will remind whoever looks at what God has done in you. You are the temple of the Lord and need to treat that privilege with reverence. The fame of the children of Israel, who conquered nation after nation, was not Moses but the Ark of the Covenant. When the enemies of Israel saw the ark, they trembled because the reputation was not of the people but of the glory present amongst them. Even the blessed people of God could not treat that glory with irreverence—the last person to lay hands on the glorious ark dropped dead.

It is a privilege, not a chore, to come to church and be in the presence of the glory. It is a privilege to serve in the ministry. It is a privilege to deal with different personalities in services of worship. It is a privilege to sit in church and be taught by and confronted with the very Word of God. It is a privilege to dance and to shout before the Lord and to give unto Him. Only the immature in spirit might be stressed by the responsibilities of being in the Kingdom: the sons count it all a privilege. The children might not feel like being bothered with all of the life renewed through Christ, while the mindset of sons is to go early for the chance to pray and to serve so everything falls into place.

Following the rules of the kingdom and abiding by the word of the King shows that you are not just a citizen, but a son. Citizens wear what they want, but sons adorn themselves under the order of their father. Citizens talk how they wish, but sons have the diction, the mannerisms, the expressions of their father. The father's honor is carried out by the son who does what is right and submissive and whose character mirrors his father's. I demonstrate honor to my father as a result of who I am and what I do. I build the family name as a son, a perpetuator of the father's legacy. As a son, I occupy the relational blessing of the father.

Finally, as a son, I inherit of my Father's substance. I am a steward of the glory. I am entrusted with the riches of my Father. In stewardship under Him, I refute ownership. I understand I own nothing but my own soul. Everything I have is subject to be given up, because I am only a steward. He will give me things temporarily until I'm ready to have real treasure entrusted to me. But I am also a son, not only a steward, so I am entrusted with His integrity, His character, His honor, and His Spirit. As a son, I am to show forth all of those things, and I have to uphold His name.

This is our greatest challenge: everything we do represents our Father to everybody around us. If we honor, tolerate, embrace, or accept anything but His Spirit and His mandates, we fall short of His glory. Holiness is the lifestyle of sons, an action and behavior, not a concept.

When you are born again, a great treasure—the glory of God—is deposited in your vessel of clay. No matter how you used your body and your mind before, even just a month ago, a great treasure comes to earth when you are born again. Are you ready to carry it? Are you prepared to demonstrate it?

Forget about wealth, acceptance, friends, and all else. You are a glory carrier. When Jesus declared, "It is finished," and dropped His head, He gave up the glory as He gave up His life. The earth quaked and the Father revealed the nature of the first carrier of glory. He ripped the veil that separated everyone from the Holy of Holies, and He will do the same for you. He does not rip the veil from the floor up, because it does not start where a man could reach: He rips it from the top down, unveiling the glory.

Soon, there will be a shouting out from within you like the rising of the sun, regardless of your personal struggles. The glory of God will blow your mind, because you never equated the depth, degree, and dimension of suffering to the revelation of the glory in you. When that glory is revealed, you won't even remember your suffering.

I want to encourage you, sons of God, whether male or female, to conduct yourselves in alignment with the unction of God, even if it is contrary to how you feel. The Spirit of God will push you to act on the glory in you and cause your mind to dwell on it. If you overanalyze, if you try to reason away the unction, your mind over spirit, then you are not behaving as a son. Reaffirm in your thoughts that you cannot exalt yourself over the revelation of the glory in you. Cast down any dissension in yourself so that you are ready to serve God only. You do not have to be in a certain situation or positive place to serve God. He does not have to change your situation for you to change your reaction. The devil will say, "You praised, you were one of the foremost worshippers, one of the foremost dancers, but it didn't help you at all." It is true that your actions may not have changed the situation, but they surely helped your spirit. You will be a better person due to your praise, your service to the Lord. You are better when you reduce yourself in your own eyes and give God His rightful place in your life.

Make the decision now, a decision independent of the continuation or arrival of anything in your life, to bless the Lord at all times and keep His praises continually in your mouth. Pray to the Father that you become a son of God at last, and place Him, to the best of your human ability, at the center of your life, that the glory He has deposited in you might shine forth with His wealth, His integrity, His character in a greater way than ever. You do not represent yourself—that's sinful, satanic in nature. You must represent the glory that lives in you, so you do not succumb to what you have felt and done many times before. Thank the Lord we are able to be led by the Spirit of God so that we are not just the *teknon*, but the heirs, the sons of God.

3 The Glory Is Here

'The glory of this latter house shall be greater than of the former,' saith the LORD of hosts: 'and in this place will I give peace,' saith the LORD of hosts (Haggai 2:9).

Change or Transformation?

The words chosen to represent an idea are important. Once, when I was talking to some people about the importance of change in the life of man, they objected that I should use the term transformation instead. From their perspective, change is not always permanent, but implies that the object can revert to its initial form. On the other hand, transformation is a phenomenon that takes places on a fundamental level and makes reverting almost impossible. When you are transformed from one state to another, you will remain in the new shape or form, because there is constancy in the genuine process of transformation that starts at the core of your being and diffuses outward, spreading to every fiber of who you are.

For instance, water undergoes change. In the space of minutes, it can turn from its solid form to liquid, and from there to gas. Under certain conditions, it can turn into and remain ice, firm and tangible, indefinitely, but when exposed to heat it melts and gives up its substantial form—yet it can always turn back again.

We are not meant to be like that in our change. We must be transformed into a new creature and not revert to our old passions and failures. When transformed by the blood of the Lamb, when indwelt by the Holy Spirit, our only transformations should be towards the better, purer things of heaven instead of back towards the ways of the world. We cannot transform backwards.

The transformation we should desire is the complete, total transformation of life and soul. We are created to be the carriers of the glory of God, and that is an enormous blessing. In Exodus

40:34, the Bible reveals the awesome presence of the Lord's glory when He descended to fill the tabernacle. The awe-inspiring image should be all the more incredible to us because under the new covenant, we become His temple and the carriers of glory.

This should radically change the way we live. Everything we do is overshadowed by His near glory. Whatever comes our way, be it difficulty or adversary, challenge or despair, we need not be moved.

For instance, I was diagnosed with diabetes. Even though the sickness is an incessant one, I refused to let it get in the way of my giving God the glory and honor He deserves. I believed He was going to heal me, but occasionally, I felt frustrated because I thought, "God, I'm Your son, not just Your child. So why, Lord, can't I declare it and it will be gone?" Recently, I had a bout of sickness that disheartened me until I realized that God had not just given me dominion in the sense that I can speak to the trial and it would be gone, but that He has given me dominion in the sense that even when my trial is present, it still has no power over me.

Through my oscillatory feelings of discouragement, I allowed the sickness to have dominion over me. Every time I indulged in frustration about my imperfect health, I only amplified its power over my mind and body. As I gave it power, I began to doubt the potency of God's power to sustain me. I would admit that God is the Healer, but then doubt whether He would want to heal me. Every time I entertained those thoughts, I gave the situation a greater hold over me. I needed time to realize that even though the sickness was present in my body, it had no lasting power over me. When I relinquished it to God and His decision, then I had freedom from struggling against it, and a holy boldness of faith arose from the fact that God was present with me.

There is an even better example of this recorded in Mark 4:35–41. Christ's followers had their own plight that resulted in a test of their faith. On that fateful day at the Sea of Galilee, when Jesus and His disciples were on a ship, a storm threatened their lives. The disciples were thrown into disarray when untimely death seemed to stare them in the face. They had forgotten that the Omnipotent was right there in the ship with them and would see them through as He willed. When they called on Him in fear, He responded, "Why are you so fearful? How is it that you have no faith?"

Having God with me means that I have more power than sickness, adversaries, or anything else could wield over me. Because God is present and I am still living and lifting my hands to give God the glory, I still have a good portion of health and strength for the time I need to continue living. The fact that I can do all I still do means that God has given me a power that this world cannot match.

This principle holds true in all situations. God wants to free us from whatever has kept us from being true carriers of His glory. Sometimes we don't always know what inhibits us from getting to where God wants us to be, but whatever the case, I declare prophetically, "If you yield to Him and only if you yield to Him, and if you give up what you have had and give Him everything you've got so He can give you everything He has, you will be transformed, not just changed."

Transformed to Bear Infirmities

The transformation that occurs in our lives is not merely for elevating us to a perfected state in the future. We are transformed for this present time so we can bear infirmities and weights while remaining glorious in Him.

Many people will not like to hear that, but the truth remains. Of course, we want God to heal and deliver us all the time, right when we think we need it, but that is not always in His plan. Yes, God can and will heal us, but there are circumstances that He needs us to bear sometimes. How do you respond when you have to face such difficulties in your life?

God needs glory carriers who shine even when things are not working out the way they would wish, who glorify Him even when things don't look right, pleasant, or comfortable. He needs carriers of glory who stand fast even when their trials are not changed or removed. God is calling on you to carry His glory. "For our light affliction, which is but for a moment, is working for us a far more exceeding and eternal weight of glory." (2 Corinthians 4:17)

Preaching a gospel that says, "Rebuke it, and it will be gone," is easy and reassuring, but God does not promise that. What He does promise is that when the end comes at last, Christ will give the victory, and whatever His true followers are going through will be defeated forever. When the end of your story comes, you will be the one shouting with victory in the name of Christ.

Even in the present, however, we still have hope. In the case of one of Apostle Paul's fellow workers, Epaphroditus, who had become gravely ill due to *"the work of Christ,"* the Lord spared him for the sake of His servants. In Philippians 2:27, Paul explains that *"he was sick nigh unto death: but God had mercy on him; and not on him only, but on me also, lest I should have sorrow upon sorrow."*

For those of you who have been down and out, who feel like God hasn't been working on your behalf, who may have concluded that your trust in God does not seem to be working for you, remember: God is right there with you in your trials. He has not left you because He cannot leave. Only your feelings have ceased to perceive Him. He will never forsake you. It may look as though He is not there, but if you continue to follow Him, you will have more of God within you than you ever had before.

47

It is worth noting that your enemy, that old serpent called the devil, is mad. He wants to put more pressure on you to keep you down and away from the Lord. The only way you can fight an enemy like that is to stand up and tell him, "Bring on the pressure, I know that I shall not be moved. I will not be moved because I am being transformed into the image of Christ, and you could not defeat Him! He is with me and you cannot overcome His love." (See Romans 8:35–39.)

The enemy can never bring anything against you that is too much for you. No matter how he attacks, he will be defeated now and in the future. For myself, God encouraged me in my sickness that I ought to stop giving up my power in Him. Before, I had been giving up all the time, even though I was asking God for power. I had pleaded with God to deliver me from my situation, but God instead taught me the lesson that He has equipped me to stand firm when I exercise my faith in Him.

Consider how even Jesus Christ had His agony at Calvary that afflicted Him horribly. He knew He had to be there, and He knew what He had to do, but once faced with the trial in the present, it became terribly real to Him. The reality of the travail and agony set in, and when the Father turned His back on Him, Jesus had to cry out in desperation, *"My God, My God, why hast Thou forsaken Me?"* (Matthew 27:46). He reached the point where even He struggled to handle the trial before Him. He had anticipated the crucifixion, but not the extent of the affliction. The Father did not give an answer, but left His Son to trust in what had to be done.

God did not reassure Jesus that it would be all right. He turned His back on Him, for our sakes, and Jesus was left to hang there without a word of comfort or assurance from the One who had sent Him into the world. Nothing came to relieve Him, but it was the greatest and most wonderful work that God had accomplished for our sakes, even though it came with unfathomable pain.

Through the crucifixion, we can twice over derive comfort for our painful situations. Not only does the death and resurrection of Jesus give us a gift of love that is more than we could ever deserve, but it also shows us that a horrible trial or a painful situation does not negate the purpose and love of God. Furthermore, if Jesus had not risen from the dead, we would have no hope that we can make it through the rigors of life. Jesus endured trouble, heartache, abuse, and death, but He eventually got up again. This suggests to me that since I am an heir of the Father and a joint-heir with Christ, I can also get up whenever I find myself in trying times, provided I endure the challenges with faith.

Survivors in the Fold

Carriers of glory are survivors. We overcome. Every now and then, we face situations that we stumble through, sometimes even crawl through, but we survive. Though we do not walk out with our heads held high, we dragged ourselves through and kept the faith. Being a survivor means that although the odds were against you—perhaps everyone and everything tried to make sure you could not make it out—you are today standing confidently where God put you.

Jesus told His disciples that the world would be against those who follow Him. If you think the present world that you see before you is all there is, the only predictable result would be that we would never receive the victory. It would look like you would never be freed of your trials, healed of your ailments, or changed from your old life forever.

God, however, tells us that there is far more than meets the eye on earth, and He wants us to stay where He puts us without falling into doubt or growing impatient. He wants us to wait for

Him to complete His work in us, that we may be transformed. When that time comes and you see what He has done, you will lift up your hands and proclaim, "Nobody is like God." Even when it looks like you couldn't make it out, God is in control and working for the revelation of glory.

Are you in a situation right now that looks as if you can't escape? Emotionally, mentally, spiritually, it looks like you aren't going to get through or be delivered. Regardless of how it appears, if you're a carrier of God's glory, there is no chance that you will not have the ultimate victory.

I refuse to continue responding to things like I used to respond, or to think the way I thought when I did not carry the glory. I want to be a different person, far better than the person that people recognize me as. Outward behavior is a manifestation of what is inside, but you can easily trick people by going through the motions. We need to submit even our minds to the Lord. For myself, I had to change my thoughts regarding my sickness, because I have realized that the state of my mind is as important as the state of my body: no matter what my body is capable of, if my mind succumbs, then so will the rest of me.

"As a man thinketh in his heart, so is he" (Proverbs 23:7). If I think that I'm sick, then I'll be sick, whether I am healthy or not. If I think that I'm better than someone else, then I will act on that, whether I am or not. If I think that I'm bound to fail, I will ruin my chances of success. Fear might hold you back from changing the way you think, but you can learn to trust that God can help you and that He wants to transform your thoughts. Tell yourself however many times you need to that you're going to get it together, to believe God. There is blessedness in changing your mind from fear and discouragement to faith, and in believing God that your expectation shall be realized, even if you don't feel it. Your feelings are immaterial; your mind, its thoughts and

imagination, should be fixed on God, not on emotions and sensations. *"Blessed are they that have not seen, and yet have believed"* (John 20:29).

The Custodians of God's Glory

Although you might not look like it on the outside, you are a carrier of glory when you are a Christian. You don't have to be a preacher or a missionary first. All you need is Jesus as your Savior and the baptism of the Holy Spirit.

Before we proceed any further, you should know the three types of the glory of God: there is the Shekinah glory, the Kabod glory, and the Doxa glory.

Shekinah. The shekinah is the divine glory, the habitation that is filled up with the very presence of God in a physical manifestation. He inhabits not only you but where you are with the unbearable glory of Himself; whenever He becomes visible, by coming down and resting in His creation, that is the Shekinah glory. The words used to describe it suggest 'dwelling,' and it harkens back to how He rules and abides in you. He takes total control of the habitation—He comes not to get a room in your heart, but to dwell in the whole of it.

The Bible describes how God inhabits the praises of Israel, which shows the extreme importance of our praising God now. When we praise Him, He will take notice. He will bring His glory to the place where we praise in earnestness.

Kabod. The kabod glory is the weighty glory that speaks of the honor, importance, and majesty of God. The basic word *kabod* is derived from means 'heavy,' and from the same word comes another word meaning 'rich.' Kabod glory describes how God is filled with an abundance of power and wondrous characteristics such as justice, goodness, mightiness, and wisdom. By this glory, we are shrouded in the weightiness of God; this is why demons and evil spirits will flee when they encounter you, because they cannot resist God's glory.

Doxa. The doxa glory is found in the New Testament, noting His divine renown and splendor. It is used to speak of the nature of God and what He does in self-manifestation. We are able to show that glory by upholding His good reputation in our lives so that those who encounter us can see that we are able to accomplish and to pull through more than what is humanly possible. That is often how people come to Christ: not because of what we say or because we take them to church, but because they can see the movement of God in our lives. They are compelled to serve the same awesome God Who is moving in your life in His glory.

These are the various ways we reference and understand the glory of God, and by them we can recognize what we experience in relation to Him. His glory is not contingent upon our situations, but upon His own nature, who He is. Passing through hard times is not a sign that His glory is not in us, even if sometimes it seems like God is not present as we face different situations. The presence of His glory is dependent upon who He is, what you believe in your heart and declare with your mouth, and whether you obey His commands.

Most times, we subconsciously believe that if things are going wrong in our lives, God must not be close. When you pass through challenges and are still able to take your stand in Christ and overcome them, then it's obvious that the glory of God is with you. If you live a holy and righteous life unto Him, then His glory will abide in you and go with you everywhere, every day. We forfeit our power too much to the enemy and even to our situations. The enemy doesn't defeat us because he has more power than we do, but because our poor mentality gives him power to wield over us. We are still naive about that which we have, and that is perhaps the most unfortunate thing about today's Church. We don't grasp the fact that we're carriers of the glory of God.

This is the day transformation needs to come, and you get to take the first step.

The Mission of God's Glory

> *Then a cloud covered the tent of the congregation, and the glory of the Lord filled the tabernacle. And Moses was not able to enter into the tent of the congregation, because the cloud abode thereon, and the glory of the Lord filled the tabernacle.* (Exodus 40:34–35).

When you study the different types of God's glory, you will discover through the Scriptures that they come to do three basic things in our lives. Exodus alone can shed light on those three:

1. The glory comes to bless us, or to sanction something for our good. Throughout Exodus, you can see that the glory often descended because God wanted to bless His chosen people. He wanted them to know that He and His glory were in the midst of the congregation, and He frequently called them to Him so He could bless and multiply them.

2. The glory comes to lead us. *And when the cloud was taken up from over the tabernacle, the children of Israel went onward in all their journeys: But if the cloud were not taken up, then they journeyed not till the day that it was taken up. For the cloud of the Lord was upon the tabernacle by day, and fire was on it by night, in the sight of all the house of Israel, throughout all their journey* (Exodus 40:36–38). The glory is not a passive presence, but one that interacts and guides.

3. Three, the glory comes to reveal the mysteries and

riches of God. When the glory passed by Moses, who was hidden in the cleft of rock, Moses was overwhelmed by the power and majesty, and immediately bowed down and worshiped (See Exodus 33 and 34).

In short, the glory comes to bless, to lead, and to reveal truth and majesty to God's children. Nevertheless, it's worth noting that we cannot simply welcome the glory and enjoy it because it feels good to know that God is with us, abiding in us. We cannot stop there or we will start regressing.

You have to ask, "God, what is this glory for? What is the purpose of Your blessing? Are You coming to lead me from where I am? Are You coming to reveal something to me?" Recently, when I prayed this prayer during the day of consecration, I felt God saying that He is coming to reveal to His people who they really are and what they are supposed to be doing. We need Him to do so: many of us have gotten stuck in our present lives and concerns and in who we want to be by our own strength.

We cannot limit Him to our own logic and understanding, because God's wisdom transcends ours. Sometimes our own logic doesn't even make sense to us—thank the Lord He is not confined by our standards. *"'For My thoughts are not your thoughts, neither are your ways My ways,' saith the Lord"* (Isaiah 55:8). We need to train the pattern of our thoughts after His mindset and be willing to follow His lead. Transform from the inside out, surrendering to His logic and His plan.

As God works in you and as you face trials, ask Him, "God, what are You trying to accomplish in me? Are You revealing what needs to be adjusted or transformed, or are You revealing who I really am? Are You directing me to where I am to go from here? Are You blessing where I am right now? Are You teaching me a new dimension of You? Where do You want me to be right now?

How do You want me to proceed in prayer right now? Where do You want me to read in the Scriptures? Am I doing Your will? Is Your glory here to let me know that I'm in the right place at the right time?"

The glory is here. It's not coming, but already here, and we have only to prepare ourselves to enter into it, live by it, and thrive in its divine essence. *"Christ in you, the hope of glory"* (Colossians 1:27b). Christ in you is the evidence of present glory: God's glory is always in the now. Don't mistake it as reserved for saints in heaven. You start living in it here on earth! Passing through good times or hard times does not matter. You partake of the suffering of Christ and rejoice that you are counted worthy to do so. Then, the Spirit of glory is upon you.

> *Beloved, think it not strange concerning the fiery trial which is to try you, as though some strange thing happened unto you: But rejoice, inasmuch as ye are partakers of Christ's sufferings; that, when His glory shall be revealed, ye may be glad also with exceeding joy. If ye be reproached for the name of Christ, happy are ye; for the spirit of glory and of God resteth upon you: on their part He is evil spoken of, but on your part He is glorified* (1 Peter 4:12–14).

4 Communicating with the Supernatural

"And Enoch walked with God: and he was not; for God took him" (Genesis 5:24). The supernatural is the bridge between God and man, which allows the manifestation of God's spiritual realm within man's corporeal realm. The supernatural occurs when what is beyond the natural world we know invades the systematic order of the physical world. Contrary to what one might expect, the supernatural does not occur when God speaks in heaven or performs His wonders there, because those things are natural in that realm.

When God leaves His spiritual realm and operates in our realm, however, that is the supernatural: God bringing His higher realm into contact with the physical world.

Because God has granted us free will, the supernatural does not simply descend upon us when He deems it necessary. We are charged with the responsibility of permitting the supernatural to enter us, of nurturing what is already given to us, and of displaying it to the world.

How do you permit the supernatural to come upon you? God wants to be sovereign in the realm of our lives, not only in heaven. He wants to demonstrate to mankind who He is so that we can know Him. To interact with us, He seeks those who will worship Him properly in spirit and in action, since He is God over the soul and the body, and once He has called and redeemed those ready to listen to Him, He indwells them.

The supernatural is foremost a relation to an existence beyond the observable universe. The spiritual realm is not able to be fully comprehended by our finite intelligence and senses. It deviates from what we consider normal and goes beyond what we are capable of. One of the pitfalls of our generation is that we put excessive effort into expressing the supernatural realm in natural terms. If through my own power I try to express how I am anointed by God, I fall short every time. It's not our job to put anointing into words or to otherwise make it understood by those who have not experienced it. The supernatural alone can express itself to an individual; your job is only to cultivate what you have.

However, the anointing of God, His supernatural connection with your heart and mind, does have a way of expression in the physical realm. For instance, how you dress exemplifies how the supernatural impacts you. Some clothes will make you uncomfortable to wear because of your anointing—but some people try to beat down the pricking of their consciences by intelligent arguments or by valuing other people's opinions and acceptance more than the prompting of the Spirit.

This is a simple example, but there are many other ways the same concept plays out in people's lives. Many people have told me that they were made a certain way, born to do or to be a certain thing, and I have said to them, "Okay, here's my question. I want you to answer this question honestly, because I don't have a hell to put you in, or a heaven to take you out of—I just want a real, honest answer: In the deepest part of you, do you really believe this is right? In the deepest part, the place you cannot smother with intellect, with reasons, with excuses, or with the speeches everyone else will use, is it right?"

"I know it isn't right," is the answer given, and that is what we should be concerned about. If you know in the deepest part of you that you are acting against what is right, then you are suppressing the supernatural and embracing what will destroy you.

You can be saved even from the temptation to embrace what has been a gray area for you. Even in uncertainty, you never act without some belief driving the action; if you suppress the word of the Lord, you will act wrongly, but if you turn to the Lord and act on what He says, then you will do right.

Do not think that there is only a holy variety of the

supernatural. The term "supernatural" encompasses that which transcends the laws of nature, as attributed to an invisible agent. The supernatural can be holy in origin, but it can also be unholy.

You can experience holy supernatural activity or demonic supernatural activity. You can partake in the activity of angels or of demons. The Holy Spirit can cause you to speak in tongues or to dance, but demonic spirits can mimic that power in what ways they are allowed. Demonic power always tries to imitate and mutilate what is God-inspired, so you cannot judge the supernatural strictly by behavior: judge it by the unction. If you have the guidance of the Holy Spirit, you will always be able to tell when an unction comes from the wrong source. A demonic spirit might make you dance, but it will also make you sit and not praise Him, or it will make you praise Him in a perverted way.

Perversion, anything that functions contrary to its initial purpose, is perhaps an even more prevalent struggle in the Church today than ever before. Our modern thinking has led us to an advanced society, but we face many perversions at the same time. God has not created a new rulebook for the 21st century. What God has said before is what He still says now, and He will continue to say it until the end of time. As Hebrews 13:8 states, He is the same yesterday, today, and forever. He is unchanging. He offers a way of redemption for those who repent, but He does not change His decrees or His morals. We cannot change God's words just because times have changed. If He said He will bless you, He will. If He says a type of lifestyle will land you in the Lake of Fire, it will land you there regardless of your reasoning and excuses.

God is all-powerful, and humans who worship Him must worship Him in all submissiveness, seeking Him with all their might. Our relationship with Him is supernatural, because He is above our realm, and therefore, the worship of Him grants permission for the supernatural to enter into us.

God works to transform your natural life and prepare you for eternity whenever you are living in the spirit. If you stay only in the natural, there is no room for God to enter. You need God in this realm, and you need to involve yourself in His realm. If you continue to reject the movement of God, you will not survive. You must invite the Spirit of God to move in you.

When you invite the glory into your life, you will find that the manifestation of God in the natural realm has two dimensions: one, our walk with God is an act of submission, and two, God walking with us is a demonstration of His mercy and grace.

First Dimension: Our Walk with God

The Bible has only two accounts of people who were said to have "walked with God." In Micah 6:8, the command to walk with God is reiterated, but only Enoch and Noah, born long before Micah's days, had earned the designation that they walked with God.

In Genesis 5:22, you find that "Enoch walked with God after he begat Methuselah," and, in Genesis 6:9, that "Noah was a just man and perfect in his generations, and Noah walked with God." After these two faithful men were mentioned, merely a chapter apart, no one else is given quite the same attribute. David was a man after God's own heart, and Abraham walked before God, but the phrasing for Enoch and Noah is unique.

The word for "walked" in the Hebrew language is halak. The word has many connotations, but one of them is "to pass away." The beautiful metaphor this suggests is that Enoch and Noah had to die to themselves in order to walk with God. No one can walk with his own interests at heart and still walk with God. If you walk with God, which is a demonstration of His merciful acceptance of you, then you have to die to yourself first.

Another definition of the word is the opposite: "live." Only through dying to yourself can you experience the life that God has for you. Enoch and Noah had to set aside their own ambitions, goals, and desires, and submit themselves instead to what God wanted. If you do the same, that does not mean you have no ambition left—it only means that your desires are in keeping with God's. You will be willing at any time, every time, to forgo what you would have done and to embrace His will. If you find yourself faced with something you want but that God does not want for you, then you will not fight God. Instead, you will surrender at once to reflect His desire for how you should live.

How, though, do you know when what you want is or is not what God wants for you? There is no real cause for doubt, because you will have to war against God to take what God does not want for you. Don't make the mistake of thinking that you can't go against God since He is in you. His Spirit does live in you, but He does not control you.

Sometimes, in fact, when what we want is in opposition to His expectations, we try to edge around every obstacle in our way, take every opportunity to bypass what He wants, and turn to anyone who will reaffirm our desire. When trying to undermine what God is telling us, we often go to the people of God in an effort to get them to reassure us and validate our attempts to get what we want. If they will not, we seek out other people who propose good reasons, even if they are not taking a godly perspective, for why we should ignore our conscience, just to make ourselves feel better about what we already know is wrong. The root of this self-deception is the opposite of what grows from the Holy Spirit: pursuing sinful behavior like this is following the spirit of the antichrist!

In the days of backsliding Israel, the Lord sent a man to stand at a pagan altar and prophesy that a king would be born who would put the idolatrous priests to death (See 1 Kings 13). The man of God had been instructed by the Lord to go home by a different route than the way he had come and to not eat before he arrived home, but a prophet met the man of God on the road and lied to him, saying that the Lord had told him to bring the man of God into his house for a meal.

The man of God did not check in with the Lord, but instead followed the prophet because that way tempted him. While they were eating, God sent word to the prophet to declare that the man of God would die that day because he had disobeyed the word of God and had chosen instead the word of man. Although this seems like an extreme case—the man of God died right away, because he had disobeyed direct instructions for his behavior after rebuking a disobedient nation—we are all doomed if we ultimately reject obedience.

If God tells you to do one thing, and those around you tell you to do another, you must choose God's way. Never obey anyone, whether an authority or a peer, who tells you to go against God. It's highly unlikely that your church leadership will contradict God's plan, but they can if they are walking outside of God's will. God does not contradict Himself, but people associated with Him can. All the same, what often frustrates people about church leadership is that they know the leadership will affirm what they don't want to hear: what God has said needs to be done.

The manner of life is another aspect of walking with God beyond dying to self and living according to His will. Enoch's reputation is not only that he walked with God, but, as found in Hebrews 11:5, "he had this testimony, that he pleased God."

How he lived, how he comported himself in life, put a smile on God's face. We sing, "I want to make You smile," but do we only mean that in church? Is our current lifestyle making God smile? Did the cumulative value of your behavior and disposition today please God?

Are you employing the excuse, "Please be patient with me, God," when you ought to have already progressed well beyond your current manner of life? No one who is hired to build a house lays a partial foundation and leaves the project there, unfinished, while acting like he is still carrying out the necessary work. You should be graduating from faith to deeper faith, from glory to brighter glory.

"He walked with God." We know very little of how Enoch lived, but we have a clearer picture of Noah's life. We know that Noah did not always do what was right, since we have the record in Genesis 9:20–27 of how he became drunk with wine. After he had escaped the Flood and had the world spread out at his feet, he erred, and as a result he was shamefully exposed.

Note that the one who saw his shame was dealt with more harshly than Noah, although both men had erred. The curse Noah pronounced on his son's descendants came true, directed by God. The Lord did not forget Noah's piety because the man had made a mistake, and He did not ignore the wrong done to His servant.

Noah's faithfulness prior to that misstep meant that God responded strongly against the wrong done to him. When you treat a child of God wrongly, you treat the Father wrongly. Everyone who walks with Him is precious to Him and worthy of protecting; if you turn on them, you turn on Him.

Walking with God means walking according to His will. Sometimes God steps back and gives you the chance to prove how you walk. After making His will known, He makes your will available to you so you can choose between them. He wants to know more than the easy answer to "Do you love Me?" He wants to see if you will obey. He doesn't want a robot, so He gives you the opportunity to act freely and confirm the love relationship you have with Him, determined by your choices.

In this dimension, you die. You don't die for one moment at the altar, but at every moment. The cost of walking with God is that whenever you come up against God in emotion, frustration, expression, or state, you must die to self. Even though He dwells in you, He does not take the opportunity to control you. Instead, He influences you and, if you walk with Him, that motivator will be strong enough that you will submit. Your submission—not how you shout or dance or speak—is proof positive that you love Him. Obedience through submission is the expression of your love.

Someone once said, "I'd rather be an usher in the Kingdom than be a master in the world." Choose God, not just at the altar, but in every moment and at every opportunity, and subject yourself to the knowledge of His will. If you don't know what His will is, then you can't say "yes" to an opportunity, no matter how good it is. "No" will serve until you know for certain.

Regardless of how great an opportunity seems, without God's guidance, you can and will stumble. When God makes you miss a chance, He has a greater one in store for you. Don't ask yourself, "How would my life be different if I had made this pivotal decision back then?" That is no longer a question you can answer in the will of God. Where you are now is what God will deal with, and He will create ways for you to take the steps He wants of you now.

If there is no way out of where you currently are, then that is a good indicator that you are where you're supposed to be. If you want another job but you simply can't get out of your current one, you're right where you should be; if you're laid off, it's time to transit. If you want another place to live, you will have the option to go if it is God's will for you to move—and so on, throughout all your life's situations. When you live by the hand of God, you trust Him to take you to where you need to go and keep you where you are meant to be as you walk with Him.

Finally, when you walk with God, you surrender your failures and transgressions to Him and let Him blot them out with His blood, so you can walk before Him in righteousness and faith, purified. You must turn your focus to Him. It's your responsibility to leave your sins behind at the altar and walk close to Him in obedience and through submission.

Second Dimension: God Walking with Us

Walking with God demonstrates His mercy. In order for Him to walk with me, He must be merciful because I am not holy enough even on my best day to compare to His standards. I am not righteous enough, strong enough, wise enough, or great enough to live up to Him. So for Him to walk with me, He must bestow mercy for my shortcomings.

The second dimension, God walking with us, shows His grace—giving us what we do not deserve after He pardoned us in His mercy. He shows us His favor as He walks with us.

In the third chapter of John's gospel, Nicodemus, a Pharisee, came to Jesus by night and spoke with Him. Though Nicodemus was a teacher of the Jews, he called Jesus "Rabbi." How is it that he called Jesus "Teacher" when he was himself supposed to be a learned one? In the presence of the real Teacher, even a well-known teacher will surrender his authority and speak as the student.

"Rabbi, we know that Thou art a teacher come from God: for no man can do these miracles that Thou doest, except God be with him" (John 3:2). Nicodemus did not say, "Except he be with God," because it is not the responsibility of a man to have the power to do wonders, but instead it is God who gives and sustains the power.

Notice that Jesus did not argue then that He was not only walking with God, but was God incarnate. He let His actions speak for themselves, met men where they were, and allowed the movement of God in each individual heart to testify to who He was. Likewise, don't let yourself be caught up in titles and names. Don't be offended if someone calls you by your given name rather than a title, such as Evangelist—humble yourself, and let God move through you as you die to the titles you think are important. Show the power of God as He walks beside you, instead of looking for glory through how people address you.

How do we come to the point where God is ready to walk with us? By the sufficient cleansing He gives us through Christ, and through our submission to staying clean in Him. Our walk has to be humble enough that we die fully to self and, when He starts walking with us, we don't bring back to life our flesh and mar His glory with our misdemeanors.

The reason God cannot yet send us where He wants us to be is because we still wallow in our disobedience and live for our own pleasures. As long as people can still vex you enough that you lash out at them, as long as people can tempt you to indulge in a habitual sin, then you are not ready for Him to walk with you, nor are you ready to bear His name before others.

The responsibility of carrying the glory of God means you must be ready to represent God to the world. There is more to it than signs, wonders, and miracles: the reputation of God is reflected in your every action. The integrity of His name is yours to guard. When unbelievers see you, they should see Him, not your old way of life. Your duty is to live as close to God as you can so that you can come as close as humanly possible to what Jesus said: He that has seen Me has seen the Father (See John 14:9). An authentic glory carrier is a reflection of the Father.

Those who claim that they are human and are unable to live that way forget that God made man in His own image, and He is able to reveal what a true human is to be. You will be most truly human when you abide in God, living in step with Him and letting Him prune the failures of the world out of you bit by bit. God alone can cover your humanity and change you into the human you were meant to be. Rejecting this is dangerous because you cannot at any time express your warped humanity without mishandling the glory you carry. In 2 Samuel 6:6–7, when Uzza mishandled the glory, he dropped dead—so we have the great responsibility to handle the glory with care, under God's rules.

We want God to use us greatly, but many of us don't want to be great in God and in His precepts. We want His greatness, but not the sacrifices that come with it. As Jesus declared, many will come to Him in the Day of Judgment and ask, "Lord, Lord, have we not prophesied in Thy name? and in Thy name have cast out devils? and in Thy name done many wonderful works?" They will receive a harsh answer: I never knew you: depart from Me, ye that work iniquity (See Matthew 7:21–23).

God is ready and waiting to walk alongside those who turn to Him, but He does not want mere lip-service. He looks for those who live within the power of the baptism of Spirit, not those who go through the motions of baptism, then gets up and live apart from God. If you're going to act foolishly, do not bring His reputation into it. If you decide to sin, you damage the integrity of His name. Drinking among alcoholics, smoking with crackheads, or fornicating with whores will damage your reputation and God's, because it shows that you care nothing for God's holiness, despite having claimed His glory and His name.

One problem with the Church is that we've lost restraint. We have conviction from the Holy Spirit, but we don't act on it or care enough anymore to restrain ourselves. That's why the Church has such a reputation for hypocrisy: those who carry the glory are irresponsible. They indulge in the pleasures of sin and view righteousness as a burden.

The privilege of a relationship with God requires responsibility from you so you may receive the support of the supernatural. The supernatural grants you three things when you submit to Him.

Salvation. The first and greatest supernatural act of God's realm invading man's is salvation. How sweet and joyful is life for those who are saved!

> *For when we were yet without strength, in due time Christ died for the ungodly. For scarcely for a righteous man will one die: yet peradventure for a good man some would even dare to die. But God commendeth His love toward us, in that, while we were yet sinners, Christ died for us* (Romans 5:6–8)

We were not righteous, we were not good, we were not worthy, but Christ died for us! Verse nine continues the thought, *"Much more then, being now justified by His blood, we shall be saved from wrath through Him."* What is the wrath of God that we have been saved from? That which is given to the children of disobedience: eternal damnation. All who chose to operate by their own power, to live only by what was in them, will face the wrath that is the unavoidable consequence of those actions, since they rejected the grace of God and the justification through Christ's blood.

Power. The second gift of the supernatural is power. *"But ye shall receive power, after that the Holy Ghost is come upon you"* (Acts 1:8a). The gift is not the Holy Ghost alone, but what the Holy Ghost gives. The gift that comes from God walking with you is the power of His Spirit.

Inherent power and ability—not muscle, but strength—is given through the Spirit. Power resides in something by virtue of its nature or by its ability to contain the power, and power is what a person or thing exerts. Power to perform miracles as well as power to stand against all the assaults of the devil comes with the Spirit. You shall lay hands on the sick, you shall have moral strength, and you shall have excellence of soul, mind, intellect, and emotion. It is not merely the power to do things in church; it is the power to live righteously in the marketplace, at home, and wherever you go. If you dance at church but you can't stop cursing, if you shout and look holy but can't stop fornicating, then you may not really have the power.

The power given by the Holy Spirit goes beyond the power and influence given by wealth and has influence even among the worldly. If you have this power, you will be influential regardless of your finances. You don't have to have tangible riches to have a substance and resource that other people will perceive. You can be poor or even broke among the wealthy and still impress them through the glory you display.

Even if no one is around you to be impressed, you still have to function as if innumerable people surround you. God always sees, and you should not take the power of the Holy Spirit lightly. Furthermore, everyone who has the Holy Spirit in them is connected to you, in kinship with you through the power given to them—your brothers and sisters in the glory. When you are in trouble, the Holy Spirit will make others pray for you, bless you, and support you, even if there is no one around to help you. When others need help, you must respond to the same call and not be caught slacking. Living with the Holy Spirit means you are never alone. You function as part of a whole, one of many, standing within an army.

Gifts. Thirdly, the supernatural gives you gifts.

For to one is given by the Spirit the word of wisdom; to another the word of knowledge by the same Spirit; to another faith by the same Spirit; to another the gifts of healing by the same Spirit; to another the working of miracles; to another prophecy; to another discerning of spirits; to another divers kinds of tongues; to another the interpretation of tongues (1 Corinthians 12:8–10).

These are the nine gifts of the Spirit, given to all those who come to salvation and walk with God. He gives liberally to every person who comes to Him.

And He gave some, apostles; and some, prophets; and some, evangelists; and some, pastors and teachers; for the perfecting of the saints, for the work of the ministry, for the edifying of the body of Christ (Ephesians 4:11–12).

God gives to those who follow Him, and He always gives enough for every situation and need, even if we do not see what He gives and why. He rains His gifts on you when you are His child, whether you realize you have them or not, and they begin functioning the moment you need them. The Holy Spirit anoints the gifts empowering you and brings them to life, and you will know it is God's handiwork since you could not do such things yourself.

Because you are a carrier of the glory, you are not limited in your resources. You have the supernatural working in you because you walk with God, allowing God to give you the gifts He has in store.

Everything, big or little, is going to be all right as long as you walk with God and He can trust you to keep walking with Him. Live in His mercy and His grace, and He can work through you and walk beside you.

You can see how He works through you in many ways. When you say something to somebody that you couldn't have known to say on your own and didn't think up on your own, but it came out of your mouth anyway, then you know in that moment God is walking with you. When a way out of the impossible appears, that is God coming to you in an hour of need and walking you through it, working with you consistently.

I'm tired of walking with God only to step away, then coming back just to step away again. He wants to walk with me daily, hourly, to give me the power and the gifts to carry me through life beside Him, and He wants the same for you. So struggle onward. Suffer through. Cry, but cry out to God for His help. Even if you fall, climb up again, because you carry His glory and He will not abandon you.

In Israel, the tabernacle was the center of life, and the twelve tribes were allotted specific places around it: three to the east, three to the west, three to the north, and three to the south. They had no choice where they wound up, but lived where they were assigned. The way the land was divided among tribes formed the shape of a cross around the tabernacle. If those living south of the tabernacle had said, "I'd rather live in the north," they would have forced others to move out of position and would have disrupted God's intentions and illustration. He was putting everything in order so that through those twelve tribes He could bring the redemption of the world, starting from Bethlehem and leading to Calvary. Our redemption was built, piece by piece, around the tabernacle.

The plan of God is bigger than your struggle or frustration. He has moved all the pieces in order already so that what is necessary will result. You are critical to the whole plan, because a chain is only as strong as its weakest link. No matter how little you are in the line of events, He can still use you in powerful ways.

As a carrier of glory, you are also a steward of the supernatural—you are not the owner of the power, but a conduit.

When you are a son of God, you must serve God and surrender yourself to His supernatural work in and through you. God does not invade your life to stay without permission, so you must respond.

In Revelation 3:20, Jesus said, *"Behold, I stand at the door, and knock: if any man hear My voice, and open the door, I will come in to him, and will sup with him, and he with Me."* He has the power to kick down the door. After all, He kicked down the gates of hell—but He never required hell to love Him. He can invade, but He desires love, and He will not force it from anyone. He anoints, He suggests, He calls, He even shuts certain doors, but He does not force.

I will not give the devil credit for every door in my life that has been shut. I will praise God for it because no door can be shut without His allowance or His intervention. My life is surrendered to Him and how He chooses to lead me forward into greater glory. I am a carrier, and I will walk faithfully with God.

5 Finish the Work

Exodus 39:32 says, *"Thus was all the work of the tabernacle of the tent of the congregation finished: and the children of Israel did according to all that the Lord commanded Moses, so did they."* In the beginning of this chapter, you'll see where God commanded Moses to build the tabernacle. He gave Moses explicit instructions on what to do, and after taking the instructions, the scripture says, *"in the second year of the same month,"* Moses began to build the tabernacle, which means that Moses took his time to do what God asked him to do.

Although Moses didn't start building right away, he did everything just the way God instructed him to without adding or leaving anything out. He simply followed God's instructions to the letter. This absolute and unalloyed attention to detail eventually led to the glory of God filling the tabernacle on its completion.

Oftentimes, the latter part of God's glory filling the tabernacle interests us so much that we fail to realize that the people of Israel, under the leadership of Moses, had made concerted and conscious efforts to do everything, absolutely everything expected of them. This is highlighted by verse 33 of the same chapter, *"Moses finished the work."* Although it is only convenient that we jump to the "juicy part" of God's glory filling us, we must, however, face the harsh reality of finishing whatever work God has committed unto us to enjoy this kind of benefit.

Don't Abandon the Work

What is it that God has required of us? What is it that God has given us explicit instructions to do? Did He tell you to get up at 5 am every morning and come before Him? Did He tell you to gather your family together and begin to pray? What did He give you instructions to do that you have not finished? Many times, we get so excited only in receiving instructions from God. Just like a kid who just got a new toy he has been yearning to have in his possession; we embrace the word, we look forward to doing just

76

as instructed every moment, we carry out each and every instruction religiously, and it is all we can think about. But along the line, the kid in us gets bored with the toy even though there is nothing wrong with it. The toy is still as new as the first day we got it, we just can't exercise the patience to complete the work He has entrusted us with, so the result of this impatience is our finding another toy, finding another commission from God.

The only setback we have in our search for another commitment is that God doesn't belong to that school of thought; He completes whatever He has started and He wants us to finish His work and complete what He told us and declared over our lives.

Have you been committed long enough for God to bless that thing He has put in your charge? Have you been doing that long enough for God to come and inhabit and fill with His glory? Have you been staying committed and obedient to that long enough for God to show up? Sad to say, many of us have not. Many of us have not been committed to what he said. Many of us have not obeyed what He said. Many of us have not even thought about what He said because it does not satisfy the flesh. The things that don't satisfy us, we're not interested in. The things that we don't think will benefit us, we're not interested in but God wants us to return to the work that he told us perhaps, a month ago, a year ago, two years ago. He wants us to go back to the work, stay in the work, commit to the work and finish the work.

I know it is not a 'convenient' gospel to preach, but I desire for you to be transformed to a state where you cannot and will not be moved. We have abandoned what He said, we have abandoned what He told us to pray about, we have abandoned what He told us to believe, and we have abandoned what He has given us to do.

Even in the church, we have abandoned the ministry that He has given us. We've abandoned the commitment that He gave us and we're expecting God to bless us, but God is telling us that He wants us to complete the work. We've abandoned our families and our marriages because it isn't working. We've abandoned doing what God said. But God has required things of us we have left and abandoned without which we may not experience the filling of his glory. We need to accept this fact to make any meaningful progress in our walk with God. We must come to the understanding that He is the Master Planner and He won't place in our hands that which we cannot handle. We need to come out of our comfort zone, most times completing His work requires our making sacrifices.

Just Do It

It is common knowledge how we strive, work our hands to the bones when we desire the worldly promotion at work, that posh car and house, that good GPA. It is this kind of attitude that we need to put into that which He has called us to do. God is saying, "Stay in and fight and don't say a word." You cannot just abandon His work just because it no longer sits well with well, just because it is not convenient for you or simply because you feel you need another challenge. I sincerely do hope we don't expect God to bless such abandoned projects. Oh! You really expect God to fill it? You expect God to overlook an incomplete work done by you? You expect God to turn a blind eye to that partial commitment to his work? God says, "I cannot bless, I cannot fill it until you finish the work." It requires a lot of faith and determination from you. You must be ready to get back up and complete the difficult things in your life.

Get to the place where you say, "Okay God, if you said it, then I'm going to declare it. I'm going to do it. God, it does not matter what it looks like, it does not matter what it seems like, it does not matter what I'm facing, and it does not matter how I feel. I will stay in this place and complete the work."

If you yield to the Master today, He is going to come and He is going to fill those works with his glory and if you commit to him today He's going to give you strength to complete what you started. We also need to change the mindset of sitting around waiting on a divine strength to come so we can complete that assignment; God is saying that it does not work that way, and being with Him for some time should have brought this realization. If you give in, then what you need will come and lift you up so you can do what He said.

Stop waiting on strength, get in it and do it. Stop waiting to feel good about it, get in it and do it. Stop waiting for your heart to be lifted, get in it and do it. Stop waiting for your mind to be changed, get in it so your mind can change about it. We are carriers of God's glory. We have to get into the action. We don't like it, but we have to get in it. I don't like getting up early in the morning but I just have to get in it and complete the work. I understand that if I complete the work, I can expect God to bless me. I don't like it, but I get up. I get in it and I get into prayer and when I get in it, I feel the strength of God coming to lift me up, but I needed to play my part of waking up, of denying myself of another minute of sleep. God won't do for us what we can do for ourselves. He's not going to shove a log of wood into our eyelids so we won't sleep. No! He's not going to do that.

Get in Place

Also, one mistake we make in our expecting God's face to shine upon us is that we expect God to bless while we are not even remotely near the place He's coming to bless. We're expecting God to bless and yet are 50 miles south of where He's meeting us to bless us; we are not even in the vicinity of His blessings.

Moses did listen to what God said and for a year he was committed to doing what God said. Perhaps, he got weary. Maybe some tools that he needed were not present at the time. Whichever

79

it is, it is certain he had to face some things that were difficult for him to continue, but he stayed in the place and he finished the work. When he finished it, verse 34 says, *"Then a cloud covered the tent of the congregation."* We can have the same testimony, we can say to ourselves and I know for sure that when we finish the work that has been committed into our hands, not because of the length, but according to God's timing, a cloud will cover the tent of the congregation and it will be said that the glory of the Lord filled the tabernacle.

God Filling the Tabernacle

"...and the glory of the Lord filled the tabernacle" (Exodus 40:34). Now this glory in this particular scripture is the *kabod* that we talked about earlier, the kabod that comes is the honor of God. It is this kabod, the weight and heaviness of God, that shows His majesty and honor that we see when we complete that assignment He has given unto us. Whatever God has given us to do; then He comes, his glory comes and shows forth His majesty, His weightiness, His heaviness, and His honor. This is important because at the end of the scripture, it says that the children of Israel went onward in all their journeys when the cloud was taken up but if the clouds were not taken up then they journeyed not till the day that it was taken up; for the cloud of the Lord was upon the tabernacle by day and fire was on it by night in the sight of all the house of Israel throughout all their journeys.

Now, the reason that the kabod was present was that God needed all of Israel to see the splendor and the majesty of God. At this moment, He didn't need them to feel the divine impartation. He didn't need them to be slain. He didn't need them to see who God is and what God does. Yet, all He needed Israel to see was that He was majestic and that He was honorable because what we equate majesty and honor with is kingship, right? We think of kings as having majesty and honor and we also think of a king as someone who can declare a word and it happens. So, this implies that God desires His weightiness to be on us. This is important as we need to make a good impression when we come in contact with people, they need to see that you have somebody fighting for you. It must be evident that you are not coming on your own. It should be clearly seen that you're not coming by yourself. The enemy needs to know that you've got the backing of the Lord, the King of kings, and the Lord of lords, the Mighty One, the Heavenly Father and He wants all of Israel and everybody in their vicinity to see His manifestation. He was so eager to show it to the Israelites so that anyone who also comes in contact with you will know who they are dealing with.

In a scenario whereby someone comes into a fight without anybody having any knowledge of who that person is say on a playground; it gives the opposition and every other person present the confidence to pick on such a person. It gives them the leeway to do all sorts of dehumanizing thing to his person. However, it's not the same reaction when such a fellow comes into a fight being known as the little sister or the little brother of so and so. When you come into a fight, and people know who you are, it changes their mentality about how they approach you. Instead of coming to beat you up, some of them might come around to see eye to eye with you on whatever the issue is because they understand that the person they are fighting or coming against has more authority than they do. You've got the name of the King, you've got the power of the King, you got the kabod of glory on, you've got that weighty and that heavy glory on you and so instead of coming to take you out, they come to join you because you possess just what they need, and you have such an influence they want to associate with.

So, God has the kabod; He comes over the tabernacle, and the Bible says, *"and Moses was not able to enter into the tent of the congregation because the cloud abode thereon and the glory of the Lord filled the tabernacle."* You see this particular verse mentions it twice. In the first verse, it says that a cloud covered the tent of the congregation and the glory of the Lord filled the tabernacle, and then it goes further to say, *"and Moses was not able to enter into the tent of the congregation because the cloud abode thereon and the glory of the Lord filled the tabernacle."* Why does God keep filling this tabernacle even though He filled it once? He filled it once; how is it that He can fill it again? God needs to continually fill every aspect of us because His glory is not just targeting a portion of our lives but wants to fill all.

Most times, we get happy because God fills the place where we are right now, but it's such a delight to know that His glory follows us everywhere we go and wherever we set our feet on. It follows us as long as we yield to the Master and as long as we complete the work, then His glory will fill every single place. He has already ordained the footsteps that we're taking. He has already ordained the direction that we tread, and that is why each time we stray away from God's designated path for us as a result of things not looking promising or going the way we want them to, we immediately get back on track because we know that our steps are ordered by the Lord. You have to know that even if it looks like you're in the same place right now, your steps are ordered by the Lord and as it is written, *"...Moses was not able to enter the tent of the congregation because the cloud abode thereon and the glory of the Lord filled the tabernacle."*

The glory of the Lord filled the tabernacle to its capacity, nor did it leave any space vacant. This word, *filled* means to be full or to have abundance in something that was lacking. It means to accomplish something so much that there is nothing empty in it. It means to fill it to the point that it's almost overflowing but it's not quite overflowing yet, but when there is a lacking, then there is more glory that fills the tabernacle. The word *filled* means to satisfy. Sometimes, we like to believe that God cannot satisfy us. We like to believe we have a lot that we want God to do and until we get what we want from God, then we cannot be satisfied. You must know that you serve a God who can satisfy you. You serve a God who can fill every place from the inside of you. Does that mean you won't have to desire anymore? No, but what it means is that while waiting on God, you are so full and satisfied in Him.

While I wait on Him to do what He said He would do, I'm so satisfied in Him that I don't need to think I can't take it anymore. When I step into satisfaction in God, I wait on Him to do what He said He would. God wants to give to us in His own season and timing. If we yield to Him today, God will undoubtedly satisfy our soul. He comes to satisfy. What does satisfy mean? Satisfy means that it quenches everything that is wanting or lacking. It means that it quenches and it brings answers to everything that you've been questioning. Satisfaction also does not mean that you get all you want at the present, but instead, it's the peace of mind, the confidence you have that you are going to surely be satisfied at the end of the day.

Have you ever been in church on a Sunday, hungry and knowing full well it's going to be one of those long services? You even look forward to that sumptuous dinner, but that's never enough to stop the rumbling in your stomach; you want an immediate fix or something that would keep you going till you have access to a proper meal. Sometimes, many of us will eat a snack. We'll get something to drink, we'll get some crackers, we'll get some almonds and what that does is, it satisfies us until we get to the place where we can receive what God has for us. God wants to satisfy us. Some of us are already in the place of satisfaction from God, and we love it, and we're enjoying it, and God desires we stay put. On the other hand, some of us have not gotten to the place where we understand that God can satisfy us.

We think that what we need is beyond God's ability; we think that God has to give us something in order to make this right, but God wants to bring us satisfaction if only we can allow Him to inhabit and dwell in our abode. God is here to fill the tabernacle, give it satisfaction, and bring it completion. He is coming to complete us, make us whole, and bring an end to our lack. Many of us are seeking for God to give us an answer but we're not seeking God to make us whole because we are afraid to let go of certain things He requires of us.

We have been functioning in less than who we are; waiting on God to take the baby steps for us. God wants us, as carriers of His glory, to carry something that would make us whole as we journey. God desires to fill us, even in places that we've been without, until He sends the miracle, the answer to where we lack. Until He sends the wonder, He does not want, neither can He afford His sons to be lacking. When we are lacking, we are a prime target for the enemy. When we are without, we are a prime target to be a casualty in war. This is the reason God wants to fill, complete and accomplish things in us. He is coming to push out, purge, cleanse, and scrape off anything in us that is not like Him. He has come to fill that black hole in us, that empty space we operate from, not because we are a lost cause or an object of empathy, but because it is our right, as *carriers of the glory!*

ABOUT THE AUTHOR

A Detroit native, Bishop Jeronn C. Williams, I, is the senior pastor and founder of the New Life International Family Church, the presiding bishop of the Breath of Life Fellowship, the chancellor of Sharing Life School of Ministry, the proprietor of JCWilliams Ministries, and co-owner of the up and coming Jeronn Authenticate clothing line. He is the devoted husband of Dr. LaToya K. Williams and the proud father of his namesake, Jeronn Cordell, II.

Spoken into existence by the late Apostle Arturo Skinner, developed under the teachings of the late Apostle Charles O. Miles, ordained to the pastorate by the late Apostle Lobias Murray, divinely inspired by the rich revelatory preaching of the late Apostle Richard D. Henton and consecrated bishop by Archbishop Lawrence Langston, Bishop Williams is commissioned to restore order according to God's original intent and purpose. He is mandated to preach a relevant Word of God through the demonstration of signs, wonders and miracles.

With a heart to serve and a tenacious spirit, Bishop Jeronn C. Williams, I, and the New Life International Family Church are determined to reach the harvest of souls throughout this world in the endeavors of Building a People...Serving the Whole Man.